From Great Men

King David of Israel

Joseph of Arimathea

Charlemagne   Charles Martel

Rollo the Viking   Alfred the Great

David I, King of Scotland   William the Conqueror

William Marshal

Robert de Ros

Front Cover Image by Robert H. Nelson and Emma L. Nelson

Robert H. Nelson
and Emma L. Nelson

From Great Men

The Famous Ancestors of
Alice de Plumpton

outskirtspress
DENVER, COLORADO

From Great Men
The Famous Ancestors of Alice de Plumpton
All Rights Reserved.
Copyright © 2012 Robert H. Nelson and Emma L. Nelson
v2.0

Outskirts Press, Inc.
http://www.outskirtspress.com

ISBN: 978-1-4327-7913-9

Library of Congress Control Number: 2012904763

Outskirts Press and the "OP" logo are trademarks belonging to Outskirts Press, Inc.

PRINTED IN THE UNITED STATES OF AMERICA

This book is dedicated to the memory of our parents,

Ray R. Nelson   **John D. Weaver**

Margaret Rosalie Swartz   **Grayce Leona Graham**

our connections to earlier generations.

"Remember the days of old, consider the years of many generations...."

Deuteronomy 32:7

Contents

Preface

Disclaimer

Chapter 1 · Robert de Ros · 13

Chapter 2 · William Marshal · 23

Chapter 3 · David I, King of Scotland · 35

Chapter 4 · William the Conqueror · 39

Chapter 5 · Rollo the Viking · 51

Chapter 6 · Alfred the Great · 57

Chapter 7 · Charlemagne · 65

Chapter 8 · Charles Martel · 77

Chapter 9 · Joseph of Arimathea · 83

Chapter 10 · King David of Israel · 107

Selected Bibliography · 135

The Authors · 138

Also Written by the Authors · 139

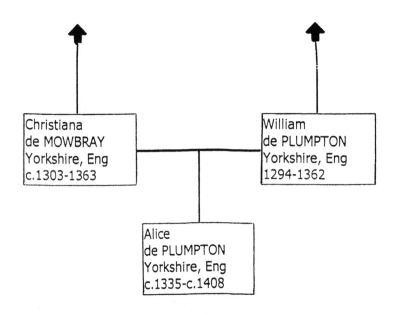

Christiana
de MOWBRAY
Yorkshire, Eng
c.1303-1363

William
de PLUMPTON
Yorkshire, Eng
1294-1362

Alice
de PLUMPTON
Yorkshire, Eng
c.1335-c.1408

Preface

Emmy Lou and I began to search for our ancestors about 1967, soon after we were married. In the years since then each of us has had many important finds.

I discovered, for example, that I am descended from <u>John Bowne</u>, a colonial leader in the American struggle for religious freedom; <u>Elizabeth Fones Winthrop Feake</u>, a niece of Massachusetts Bay Colony Governor John Winthrop and the fascinating woman portrayed in the highly acclaimed historical novel, *The Winthrop Woman,* by Anya Seton; <u>John Chew</u>, the founding member of a founding family of Virginia; <u>Dr. Thomas Wynne</u>, the personal physician for William Penn on his voyage to Pennsylvania on the *Welcome* in 1682, the speaker for the first two Pennsylvania Assemblies, and a direct descendant of Charlemagne and medieval royalty; and <u>James M. Corns</u>, the commander of the 8th Virginia Cavalry Regiment of the Army of the Confederate States of America. (James M. Corns was the subject of our book entitled *James M. Corns: The Ancestry and Life of a Warrior* which was published in 2009.)

Another discovery that I have made is that I am descended from <u>Alice de Plumpton</u>. That discovery has led to learning about her ancestral lines which have proven to be remarkable, to say the least.

Alice de Plumpton was a relatively obscure member of a well-known aristocratic family in Yorkshire, England. She was born about 1335, the daughter of William de Plumpton and his wife Christiana de Mowbray. Her father held important positions including that of High Sheriff of Yorkshire, and he was knighted in 1340. Alice de Plumpton became the wife of Richard de Sherburne in 1352. The ancestry of Alice de Plumpton included knights, kings, queens, emperors, crusaders, Magna Charta Surety Barons, religious and military leaders, and other prominent historical figures.

Each of the chapters in this book, *From Great Men: The Famous Ancestors of Alice de Plumpton*, describes a very famous and influential person of history: <u>Robert de Ros</u> (Magna Charta Surety Baron), <u>William Marshal</u> (the greatest knight in all of history and the Protector of England), <u>David I</u> (King of Scotland), <u>William I of England</u> (William the Conqueror), <u>Rollo the Viking</u> (the first leader of the Normans), <u>King Alfred the Great</u> (the maker of England), <u>Charlemagne</u> (the Emperor of the West), <u>Charles Martel</u> (the warrior who saved western civilization), <u>Joseph of Arimathea</u> (a great-uncle of Jesus, and his guardian after the death of Joseph "the carpenter"), and <u>King David of Israel</u> (the originator of the prestigious Davidic Bloodline and a favorite of God and human rulers alike). One thing these great men had in common was that they were all direct ancestors of Alice de Plumpton.

Each chapter of this book will include a chart showing the direct descent of Alice de Plumpton from the subject of the chapter. Also, we have presented, in each of the chapters, the conclusions we have reached after extensive research and study. It is important to point out that, regarding Chapters 9 and 10, there will be disbelievers and skeptics among the readers of this book, and the authors understand that. The conclusions that have been reached and presented are based on relatively unknown historical facts, and those conclusions may be difficult for some to accept since they differ from what many were taught to believe.

In Chapter 9, besides depicting the life of Joseph of Arimathea, we have presented our research findings concerning his beliefs about Jesus which will shock the reader just as the beliefs of the later Christians would have shocked Jesus. It is clear that in the years following the crucifixion Paul and his supporters began, and all the churches continue to this day, a belief system tainted by paganism that Jesus would have condemned.

In Chapter 10, besides depicting the life of King David of Israel, we have presented the exciting story of how his bloodline was transferred to the British Isles in order that there would always be a descendant of David on his throne in line with prophecy. This involves the amazing story of the role of the prophet Jeremiah who carried out God's plan to save the last remaining royal descendant of the line of David at that time (also an ancestor of Alice de Plumpton), so that the Throne of David would last forever.

The information in all of the chapters of this book has been presented as we have determined it to be the truth. The authors expect that many of the readers of this book will find this information and our conclusions so new and intriguing that further reading and inquiry will be initiated by those readers. As we have determined what is true during our research we have been anxious to present that information to our readers. The goal of getting to the truth is what has driven us to read, analyze, discard, compile, test, discuss, challenge, and ultimately write.

I want to thank Emmy Lou who has made this book possible with her great research, writing, editing, and artwork talents, and with her genealogical and historical instincts and experience.

It is my hope that we have made history come alive as we show how Alice de Plumpton, of Yorkshire, was descended *From Great Men*.

Robert H. Nelson

Disclaimer

This book has been written to convey the results of genealogical and historical research which was done by the authors. It represents the interpretations and opinions of the authors after their thoughtful analysis of the research findings.

While every effort has been made to ensure that the contents of this book (including the conclusions reached) are historically accurate, it is possible that there could be inadvertent typographical or other errors that were made during its production.

1

Robert de Ros

Alice de Plumpton had six direct ancestors who were Magna Charta Surety Barons. The Magna Charta Surety Barons were twenty-five powerful and influential noblemen who were selected to ensure that King John of England would abide by the Magna Charta.

Early in the thirteenth century the English barons were threatening civil war because of King John's abuses of his royal powers. His military failures and his ceding of territory to the pope had increased the burden of taxes onto a smaller number of taxpayers. In 1215 many of those rebelling barons met with the king and his councilors at Runnymede. The barons agreed to support the king if he would agree to the reduction of his powers and a return to the way of governing that had prevailed before the Normans had conquered England. An agreement was reached between King John and the barons.

King John of England is pictured signing the Magna Charta on June 15, 1215 at Runnymede. (Wikimedia Commons)

This agreement was facilitated by William Marshal, who was a close advisor to the king and also trusted by the other barons. (William Marshal is another ancestor of Alice de Plumpton and the subject of Chapter 2 of this book.) The document known as the Magna Charta recorded in Latin the terms agreed to at Runnymede.

The Magna Charta has great significance because it legitimized the attempt to limit the power of the king and protect the rights of the ruled. It is regarded as the basis of many of our modern freedoms and rights. In fact, the United States Constitution includes some wording identical to that in the Magna Charta.

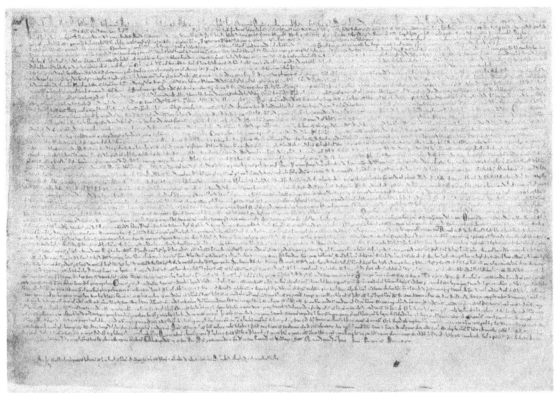

One of four known surviving 1215 A.D. exemplars of the Magna Charta, this one is held at the British Library.
(Wikimedia Commons)

The Magna Charta was signed (or, as some historians believe, the king's approval was designated through the use of his seal), and the barons renewed their vows of loyalty to the king. Included in the Magna Charta was a clause which attempted to guarantee the king's compliance. It established that a group of twenty-five barons could meet and decide to overturn a decision of the king, by means of seizing some of his properties. The individuals selected to have that power were the Surety Barons.

THE 25 BARONS APPOINTED
TO ENFORCE THE OBSERVANCE OF MAGNA CHARTA
AT BURY St EDMUND'S NOVr 20TH A.D. 1215.

NAMES.	TITLES.	BY WHOM NOW REPRESENTED.
1. RICHd de CLARE	EARL of CLARE & HERTFORD	TITLES EXTINCT.
2. GILBERT de CLARE his Son	EARL of GLOUCESTER	
3. WILLm de FORTIBUS	EARL of ALBEMARLE	EXTINCT.
4. GEOFFREY de MANDEVILLE	EARL of ESSEX & GLOUCESTER	DIED WITHOUT ISSUE
5. SAHER de QUINCY	EARL of WINCHESTER	EXTINCT.
6. HENRY de BOHUN	EARL of HEREFORD	EXTINCT.
7. ROGER BIGOD	EARL of NORFOLK	THE DUKE of NORFOLK
8. HUGH BIGOD his Son		
9. ROBt de VERE	EARL of OXFORD	THE DUKE of ST ALBANS
10. Wm MARSHAL the Younger	EARL of PEMBROKE	NO ISSUE
11. ROBT FITZ-WALTER	Marshal of the Barons' Army	IN ABEYANCE
12. EUSTACE de VESCI	BARONY	EXTINCT
13. Wm de HARDELL (or Hardel)	LORD MAYOR of LONDON	
14. Wm de MOWBRAY	BARONY	IN ABEYANCE (Lord PETRE & others)
15. GEOFFREY de SAY	BARONY	
16. ROGER de MONTBEGON		
17. Wm d' HUNTINGFIELD	BARONY	EXTINCT
18. ROBt de ROOS		LORD de ROOS
19. JOHN de LACY	EARL of LINCOLN	EXTINCT
20. Wm de ALBINI	BARON of BELVOIR	LORD de ROOS
21. RICHd de PERCY		
22. WILLm MALET		
23. JOHN FITZ-ROBERT		
24. Wm de LANVALLEI		
25. RICHd de MONTFICHET		

This inscription on the ruins of the Abbey of Bury St. Edmunds lists the 25 Surety Barons. (Wikimedia Commons)

Richard de Clare

One of the Surety Barons was Richard de Clare, a fourth great-grandfather of Alice de Plumpton.

Richard de Clare

Gilbert de Clare

Richard de Clare

Rose de Clare

John de Mowbray

Christiana de Mowbray

Alice de Plumpton

Richard de Clare was born about 1153 in Hertford, England, the son of Roger de Clare and Maud de St. Hilary. He was both the Earl of Hertford and the Earl of Clare. He married Amice FitzRobert, Countess of Gloucester. They had several children, but were separated by the pope for a while because of consanguinity. Earl Richard de Clare, having previously been loyal to King John, sided with the rebelling barons at the time of the Magna Charta. He was one of the barons called upon to negotiate peace with the king both before and after the signing of the Magna Charta. He was excommunicated by the pope because of his rebellion against the king. He died in 1218.

Gilbert de Clare

Earl Richard de Clare's oldest son, Gilbert, a third great-grandfather of Alice de Plumpton, was also a Surety Baron.

Gilbert de Clare

Richard de Clare

Rose de Clare

John de Mowbray

Christiana de Mowbray

Alice de Plumpton

He was born about 1180. Gilbert de Clare was the Earl of both Hertford and Gloucester. After the signing of the Magna Charta, King John refused to comply with the Charter. The Barons' War resulted. Louis of France joined with the barons, and they prevailed against King John. Louis was proclaimed King of England. However, he was never crowned. After King John died in 1216, popular support in England was for his heir, nine-year-old Henry III, to be king. Earl Gilbert de Clare, with his father, had been excommunicated by the pope in 1215. He then championed Louis of France during the Barons' War, and even continued that support after the death of King John. Fighting with Louis, against the forces of King Henry III, Gilbert de Clare was taken prisoner by William Marshal in 1217. Later, that same year, he married Isabel, the daughter of William Marshal. They had several children. After he joined forces with Henry III he participated in, and led, expeditions against the Welsh. He died in 1230 following a battle in Brittany.

John de Lacy

Another of the Surety Barons was John de Lacy, a third great-grandfather of Alice de Plumpton.

John de Lacy

Maud de Lacy

Rose de Clare

John de Mowbray

Christiana de Mowbray

Alice de Plumpton

John de Lacy was the oldest son of Roger de Lacy and Maud de Clare. He was born about 1192. He was hereditary constable of Chester and seventh Baron of Halton Castle. At the time of the Magna Charta he was one of the first barons to rebel against King John and was excommunicated by the pope. Following King John's death he joined other noblemen in a crusade to the Holy Land, where he distinguished himself at the Siege of Damietta. John de Lacy married Margaret de Quincy, and they had a son and a daughter. He became Earl of Lincoln because of his marriage to Margaret and, later, governor of Chester and Beeston Castles. He died in 1240.

William de Mowbray

William de Mowbray, another third great-grandfather of Alice de Plumpton, was also a Surety Baron.

> William de Mowbray
>
> Roger de Mowbray
>
> Roger de Mowbray
>
> John de Mowbray
>
> Christiana de Mowbray
>
> Alice de Plumpton

He was born about 1174, the oldest son of Nigel de Mowbray and Mabel de Clare. He was angered by the payments he was forced to make over the years to King Richard I, and then to his successor, King John. William de Mowbray married Agnes d'Aubigny, and they had two sons. William de Mowbray was governor of York Castle at the beginning of the Barons' War. He did not hesitate to side with the barons against King John. He was excommunicated by the pope because of his stand against the king. Even after King John's death he continued to fight, and was taken prisoner in the Battle of Lincoln. At that time his lands were confiscated, but he was able to get them back later and then supported King Henry III, King John's successor. He died at Axholme Castle in 1222.

Saher de Quincy

Saher de Quincy, a fifth great-grandfather of Alice de Plumpton, was another Surety Baron.

> Saher de Quincy
>
> Robert de Quincy
>
> Margaret de Quincy
>
> Maud de Lacy
>
> Rose de Clare
>
> John de Mowbray
>
> Christiana de Mowbray
>
> Alice de Plumpton

He was born about 1155, the son of Robert de Quincy and Orabilis of Leuchars. Saher grew up in Scotland. His father was a knight serving King William I of Scotland, and his mother was an heiress to a Scottish lordship. Saher, himself, gained extensive military experience as a knight. He married Margaret de Beaumont, and they had six children. As a result of his wife's position and inheritance Saher was named the Earl of Winchester and became a very prominent military figure in England. He joined with the other barons in rebelling against King John, and was one of the negotiators of the terms of the Magna Charta, as well as a Surety Baron. He was also excommunicated by the pope. Saher de Quincy was a proponent of having Louis of France become King of England, and he continued this support even after King John's death. When he and the other barons were defeated by the forces of Henry III, he was among those taken prisoner and his properties were seized. Those estates were returned to him after he submitted. Saher de Quincy, then, departed with other noblemen to join the Fifth Crusade to the Holy Land. His oldest son Robert joined him on the Crusade. They participated in the Siege of Damietta in 1219. Earl Saher de Quincy became ill and died on the way to Jerusalem later that same year.

Robert de Ros

Another Surety Baron ancestor of Alice de Plumpton, one of her third great-grandfathers, was Robert de Ros.

Robert de Ros

William de Ros

William de Ros

Lucy de Ros

William de Plumpton

Alice de Plumpton

As with the other barons, his power and influence were largely a result of the family into which he was born and the family into which he married. Robert de Ros's ancestry can be traced back to Piers, a feudal baron living at the beginning of the twelfth century who assumed the surname Ros because he lived in Ros, Holderness, Yorkshire. Piers de Ros married Adeline, an heiress to the Lordship of Helmsley. They had a son Robert, born in 1117, who then became the successor to the Lordship of Helmsley, as well as to the de Ros barony. He was the grandfather of Robert de Ros, the Surety Baron. The titles and properties were passed on to each new generation. Additional lordships were assumed through marriage. With additional property came more power. By the time Robert was born the de Ros family had already become wealthy and influential, possessing land in Yorkshire and in Normandy.

Robert was born in Ros, Holderness, Yorkshire. He was the son of Everard de Ros and Rose de Trusbut. Everard died when Robert was about fourteen years old. It was the custom that when property was inherited the heir had to pay a livery fine to the king. Robert paid his tax to King Richard I, the first king under whom he served. His prominence increased after King John's accession to the throne. He was highly regarded by the king, and was given both responsibilities and rewards for his loyal service to the king. He was made sheriff of Cumberland, and he became an even larger property holder by obtaining land in Northumberland where he built a castle at Werke. One of his duties was to travel to Scotland with other barons to escort the king of the Scots into England to pay homage to King John. He was one of the many noblemen present as witnesses when the two monarchs met on the hill near Lincoln.

During his stay in Scotland he had met and fallen in love with Isabella, the beautiful illegitimate daughter of William I, The Lion, King of Scotland, and his mistress, Isabel Avenal.

William I, The Lion, King of Scotland was the fourth great-grandfather of Alice de Plumpton.

William I, The Lion, King of Scotland

Isabella of Scotland

William de Ros

William de Ros

Lucy de Ros

William de Plumpton

Alice de Plumpton

Isabella of Scotland was the widow of Robert de Brus. Isabella and Robert de Ros married and had two sons, William de Ros and Robert de Ros.

William I, The Lion, King of Scotland and father-in-law of Robert de Ros, reigned for forty-nine years, from 1165 to 1214.

William I, The Lion, King of Scotland, shown here, was the father-in-law of Robert de Ros. (Wikimedia Commons)

Robert de Ros continued in his allegiance and service to King John during the early part of the conflict between the king and the barons, but by the time of the Magna Charta he had become a leader of the rebelling barons, and was one of the twenty-five Surety Barons. After King John's death Robert gave his support to the king's heir, Henry III. The properties he had lost during his stand against King John were returned to him, and he remained a prominent supporter of King Henry.

Robert de Ros and his ancestors were great benefactors of the Knights Templar, having donated various properties to them over the years. When Robert died in 1227 he was buried in the Temple Church in London. The type of monument there, in the form of a cross-legged effigy, indicates that he was an Associate of the Temple. Being a pious person of wealth and nobility, he was admitted into a spiritual association with the order, without having to take the vows and renounce his secular way of life.

Robert de Ros was born into a noble and respected family. Through his own accomplishments, his alliances, his service under three kings of England, and his marriage to the daughter of the King of Scotland he increased his family's prominence and fortune. As a Magna Charta Surety Baron he made a significant contribution to history by participating in events that initiated the long process that would ultimately result in our modern concepts of liberty and constitutional government.

2

William Marshal

William Marshal, known during his lifetime as William the Marshal, was one of the most highly regarded and influential individuals of medieval times. William was a strong and courageous knight, whose character, personal integrity, and wisdom enabled him to become a powerful baron with vast landholdings, a trusted advisor to four kings, and protector of the English realm. He was one of Alice de Plumpton's fourth great-grandfathers, and was one of Alice de Plumpton's ancestors on both her mother's side (Christiana de Mowbray) and her father's side (William de Plumpton).

William Marshal	William Marshal
Isabella Marshal	Isabella Marshal
Richard de Clare	Avicia de Clare
Rose de Clare	Robert de Plumpton
John de Mowbray	Robert de Plumpton
Christiana de Mowbray	William de Plumpton
Alice de Plumpton	

The surname Marshal derives from the office of marshal to the king. It originated from the French word *marechal* meaning horse servant. In twelfth century England the marshal was in charge of the military aspects of the royal household. He managed the stables and knights and records pertaining to them, and also was given minor landholdings of his own to oversee. William's grandfather, Gilbert, was marshal to Henry I, King of England. It was at that time that the office became hereditary, which led ultimately to the Marshal surname.

Gilbert's son, John FitzGilbert, inherited the position of marshal to the king when his father died. After John had served in this office for several years King Henry I died in 1135, and both the king's daughter Matilda and his nephew Stephen claimed the throne. (Matilda and Stephen shared a common grandfather, William the Conqueror, Matilda descending through his son Henry, and Stephen descending through his daughter Adela.) Stephen ascended to the throne, but Matilda contested his right. Matilda had been married to the Holy Roman Emperor Henry V, and thus had the title of Empress. A civil war broke out, making it necessary for the barons to choose sides. John FitzGilbert at first pledged his allegiance to Stephen, but later swung his support to Empress Matilda. Stephen's popular support, however, was greater, his forces proved to be stronger, and he prevailed.

John FitzGilbert married twice. He had two sons by his first wife, then had that marriage annulled so that he could enter into a strategic marriage with Sybilla FitzWalter that would improve his standing and security. John and Sybilla had several sons and daughters. Their second son was William, the subject of this chapter. William was, then, the fourth son of a minor baron.

William was born about 1147 during the period when his father, John FitzGilbert, and the other barons were engaged in the civil war to determine whether King Stephen or Empress Matilda would rule England. By 1148 Empress Matilda had left England and returned to Normandy, but her supporters continued the fight against King Stephen.

These were difficult times for John FitzGilbert. He was fighting against more powerful forces in what was becoming more and more a losing battle. During one conflict in 1152 King Stephen was besieging Newbury Castle, a fortress that John was defending for Empress Matilda. Realizing that he did not have enough supplies and men to withstand the siege, John asked for a truce so that he could notify the empress to get official permission to negotiate the surrender. King Stephen agreed, but John's young son, William, was given as a hostage to ensure that John would keep his word. Instead of keeping his promise, John used the time of the truce to add provisions and additional warriors to fortify the castle. When King Stephen returned and demanded the surrender of the castle, John refused. The king threatened that he would hang William, to which John replied that the king could do whatever he wanted to William because he (John) could produce an even better child. King Stephen, however, could not bring himself to kill the young child and instead ensured the safety of his young hostage by taking him into his household until his later release to his own family. King Stephen died in 1154 and, as had been previously arranged, Empress Matilda's son succeeded to the throne and became King Henry II of England.

John FitzGilbert was once again able to return to his position as marshal to the king.

Since William was not the oldest son he was not first in line to inherit the marshalship and holdings of his father, and so it was necessary for him to prepare a means of providing for his own livelihood. When he was about twelve years old he was sent to live with his father's cousin, William of Tancarville, who was the Chamberlain of Normandy. In his household young William served as a squire and was taught the skills and code of behavior necessary for a knight. His apprenticeship lasted through most of his teenage years. William was knighted by Lord Tancarville in 1166, at a time when the Chamberlain had been called upon to join with other forces of King Henry II of England to repel the attacks of those representing King Louis VII of France. William's first battle as a knight took place at Drincourt, and his forcefulness and fearlessness won him the respect of Lord Tancarville and the villagers who witnessed his actions. During the battle he became surrounded by about a dozen warriors who attempted to pull him from his horse. He kept fighting vigorously and was able to keep from being defeated. Although he lost his horse from wounds inflicted during the battle and neglected to capture any horses or knights, William demonstrated during that skirmish the strength, skill, and determination that would contribute to his success as a knight.

Shortly after that battle the two kings, Henry II of England and Louis VII of France, ended their war; and an era of relative peacefulness began. In the absence of actual war the knights participated in tournaments in order to stay in fighting condition and develop their combat skills. William took part in his first tournament in 1167, and from the beginning he excelled. The tournaments were imitation battles, but the fighting was very real. Working in teams the knights fought each other in attempts to capture the other side's knights, horses, and armor.

It was a very rough and dangerous activity with injuries being common and fatalities occasionally occurring. At the conclusion of one of the tourneys William had to enlist the help of a blacksmith in order to remove his helmet. Although he had won the tournament his helmet had become misshapen and stuck on his head as a result of the hard blows his head had received. The tournaments enabled successful knights to make a good living. In addition to the prize money awarded to the winners, horses could be seized and ransoms

This early drawing depicts William Marshal at a tournament as he unhorses his opponent. (Wikimedia Commons)

could be obtained for captured knights. William very quickly became the dominant knight at the tournaments. His courage, physical strength, and ability to develop successful strategies for fighting enabled him and those who fought with him to prosper. William's reputation and fortune grew as he traveled from one tourney to another.

Soon after William began to participate in tournaments he left the household of his older cousin, Lord Tancarville, in Normandy, and returned to England where he went into the service of his mother's brother, Patrick, Earl of Salisbury. The Earl of Salisbury was a friend of King Henry II of England, and was responsible for ensuring the safety of the king's wife, Eleanor of Aquitaine. While attempting to defend Eleanor, William and his uncle (the Earl of Salisbury) were attacked along the road. The Earl of Salisbury was killed and William was injured and captured. Eleanor paid the ransom for William's release.

In 1170 King Henry II had his oldest son, also named Henry, crowned as king. Although Henry II continued to rule England, his son became Henry the Young King. William's fame as a knight was so great by then that he was appointed to the Young King's household, where he was in charge of young Henry's military training. For the next twelve years William was a close companion, as well as a tutor and defender, of the young Henry. It was William who actually knighted Henry. Rather than having the knighthood conferred by a noble of high rank, the Young King chose

William whom he considered to be "the best knight that ever was or will be."

William was the ideal mentor, because he epitomized what a knight should be. His physical strength and success in combat were not the only aspects of this. He practiced in his own life the chivalry of knighthood, the moral and social code of conduct to which all knights were expected to aspire. This unwritten code of conduct included the virtues of loyalty, courage, fairness, generosity, and gallantry towards women.

Together William and the Young King led a group of other knights and participated in tournaments. Also during that period William teamed up with Roger de Gaugie, another knight in the Young King's household. Together the two knights traveled from tourney to tourney with great success. William's reputation continued to grow as he was able to continually overwhelm his opponents, and he was both respected and feared by his competitors. During those years of participating in tournaments William defeated a total of about five hundred knights.

He was renowned for his character as well as his ability to win tournaments. Henry the Young King accumulated many debts as he traveled with his entourage from tournament to tournament. The general practice was that a baron in his party would offer himself as surety for the payment of the debt. Some tradesmen would not accept this arrangement as a guarantee, but they would all accept William's word. If William said that the king's debt would be paid, it was known that the promise would be kept.

Henry the Young King and his brothers revolted against their father, King Henry II. They were motivated by their desire for land, and they were encouraged in their rebellion by their mother, Eleanor of Aquitaine. Eleanor and her husband, the king, were in conflict with each other. In fact, King Henry II had Eleanor kept in confinement for about fifteen years. The king had various mistresses, and in addition to the children that Henry and Eleanor produced, Henry II had illegitimate children. (Alice de Plumpton is descended from King Henry II through his illegitimate son William Longespee the Earl of Salisbury.)

King Henry II

William Longespee

Ida Longespee

Maud de Beauchamp

Roger de Mowbray

John de Mowbray

Christiana de Mowbray

Alice de Plumpton

The sons of Henry and Eleanor, with Eleanor's support, fought to overthrow their father and take over vast holdings. William loyally supported Henry the Young King in his revolts against his father, but Henry II was able to withstand the uprisings.

In 1183 the Young King died. Before his death he had taken a crusader's vow, but he became ill before he was able to travel to the Holy Land. As William sat with his friend, the dying king, he promised to carry his cross to Jerusalem and complete his vow for him. William went on crusade soon after Henry the Young King died. He remained in Jerusalem serving King Guy for several years. While there, he fought beside members of the Knights Templar.

This drawing of Knights Templar is from the 13th century. (Wikimedia Commons)

The Order of the Temple was a military and religious order established in the early twelfth century for the purpose of protecting pilgrims who were traveling to the Holy Land. It was founded by nine knights who had participated in the First Crusade. The king of Jerusalem gave them a meeting place on the Temple Mount, which was an area believed to be on top of the ruins of the Temple of Solomon. It was from the Temple of

Solomon that they got their name, the Poor Knights of Christ and of the Temple of Solomon, or the Knights Templar. The Knights Templar became highly skilled and respected warriors, but some members of the order worked in other roles. They protected the pilgrims by developing a type of banking system which eliminated the need for the travelers to carry their money with them. The Knights Templar were also involved in construction projects. As the fame of the Order of the Temple grew, more and more knights joined them. Each individual knight wore a white robe with a red cross and took an oath of poverty. The organization itself, however, prospered financially because many of its supporters donated money and lands though they were not ready to accept the vows themselves.

William returned from the Holy Land and entered the service of Henry II, King of England. He demonstrated the same faithfulness to Henry II that he had exhibited toward his son, the Young King. He assisted the king in withstanding the assaults of his remaining sons. On one occasion Richard, seeing an opportunity to capture his father, rode out in such haste that he didn't put on his armor. William discovered what Richard was trying to do and charged directly toward him. Richard pleaded with William to spare his life since he was unarmed, and William complied, but did kill his horse. Thus, William became the only knight to ever unhorse Richard the Lionheart. William became a trusted counselor and friend to Henry II, as well as a loyal knight. The king rewarded William for his service by giving him land and estates and offering him two different marriages, both of which William turned down. As the old king was dying he promised to give William the hand and estates of Isabel de Clare, but no official arrangements were made before Henry II died in 1189.

Isabel de Clare, a ward of King Henry II, was the extremely wealthy and attractive young heiress of Richard Strongbow de Clare. The original de Clare family held lands and titles in Normandy and Wales. When Gilbert Strongbow de Clare died in about 1148 his eighteen year old son, Richard Strongbow de Clare, inherited lands in Normandy, the Lordship of Striguil, and the Earldom of Pembroke. However, when King Stephen died and Henry II became king in 1154 he refused to recognize those titles and holdings. Richard Strongbow de Clare was a knight and baron from one of the most respected old families of the time, but he was out of favor with the king. That situation continued for about fifteen years, until Strongbow agreed to lend his support to Dermot MacMurchada in his attempt to regain his Lordship of Leinster in Ireland. Dermot promised to give Strongbow lands in Ireland, the hand of his daughter Eve in marriage, and the inheritance of the Lordship of Leinster (land encompassing about one-fourth of Ireland) when Dermot would die. Strongbow and his forces were extremely successful in assisting Dermot, and were able to take control of part of Ireland. Strongbow married Eve, and once again was a titled landholder. He also gained favor with King Henry II by helping him to defeat his sons who were rebelling. Richard Strongbow de Clare died in 1176. He and Eve had a young son and daughter by then. Their son died several years later while still young, and so their daughter became Strongbow's heir. That daughter was Isabel de Clare, and she and her father's land were extended royal protection.

When King Henry II died his son Richard ascended to the throne. Richard the Lionheart, whose life William had spared during one of the sons' revolts against Henry II, enlisted William to enter his service. That same year, in August of 1189, William married Isabel de Clare, as had been promised. William was about forty-three years old and Isabel was seventeen. As a result of his marriage to Isabel, William became one of the wealthiest and most powerful men in the kingdom, owning land in England, Normandy, Wales, and Ireland.

This is a current view of Pembroke Castle and the Pembroke River. (Wikimedia Commons)

During the reign of Richard the Lionheart William had many opportunities to demonstrate that his leadership abilities extended well beyond military matters. He and his wife managed and made improvements to their many estates and properties, renovating existing structures and building new castles. William assisted in governing King Richard's realm while he (the king) was on crusade. After the death of William's older brother, the hereditary position of marshal was passed on to William. When Richard the Lionheart returned from the crusade, William fought with him in Normandy for several years in his battles against King Philip Augustus of France. Then shortly before Richard the Lionheart died in 1199 he appointed William to be constable of the castle of Rouen, which held the royal treasury.

King Richard's brother John succeeded him to the throne. William extended his support to the new king and, in fact, was influential in assuring that John (rather than his nephew Arthur) became the next king. William held positions of great power and influence, and he was King John's most trusted advisor. In addition to carrying out the responsibilities inherent to the powerful positions he had assumed, during those years William and his young wife were building their family. They had ten children, five sons (William, Richard, Gilbert, Walter, and Anselm) and five daughters (Matilda, Eve, Isabel, Joan, and Sibilla).

King John's reign was a troubled one. His military failures, his surrender of England and Wales to papal authority, and his increasing demands for financial backing caused him to lose the support of almost all of his barons. The barons felt that the king was abusing his power, and they were threatening civil war. King John even had a major dispute with William because of William's dealings with King Philip II of France. After Philip defeated King John and conquered Normandy William was able to retain his own personal lands in Normandy by paying homage to King Philip. Because he had expressed his fealty to the King of France he would not continue to participate in John's battles against Philip. This angered John, and he caused problems for William, confiscating some of his properties and even taking two of his sons hostage. At one time William was summoned from Ireland to England by King John, providing an opportunity for one of the king's justiciars to attempt to take over William's lands in his absence. However, Isabel successfully withstood the attack against their castle in Ireland. Throughout those troubles William remained true to his code of chivalry and, although he would no longer take up arms against King Philip of France, as John's vassal he did not waver in his loyalty to his king. That support was critical to King John's survival during the barons' uprisings.

William was trusted and respected by the barons opposing the king, and he served as a mediator between the king and the barons. In 1215 William accompanied King John to Runnymede where the rebelling barons were demanding concessions from the king in exchange for their support.

William was sympathetic to the barons' concerns. In fact, one of his own sons was one of the rebelling barons at Runnymede. William and Stephen Langton, the Archbishop of Canterbury, were instrumental in convincing John that he should consider the barons' demands. An agreement was reached, wherein the king would relinquish some of his power and guarantee certain rights to his barons. The barons, in return, would renew their oaths of allegiance to the king. Twenty-five barons were selected to serve as Surety Barons. William's son, William the Younger, was one of those. The terms of the agreement were recorded in Latin and became known as the Magna Charta. William Marshal was the individual who wielded enough influence with both sides to make it possible.

The Magna Charta of 1215 has great historical importance because it became the pattern for many future documents, and is considered to be the basis of modern protections against the power of government. However, the Magna Charta was not successful in achieving its original objective of resolving the differences between King John and the barons. King John did not abide by the terms enumerated in the Magna Charta, and the Barons' War resulted. The oldest son of the king of France, who would later become King Louis VIII, lent his support to the barons. King John became embroiled in a war against his barons and the French forces. Throughout this conflict William remained loyal to King John and did not join with the rebelling barons. He led King John's military forces against the barons, one of whom was his own son, William the Younger. About one year after the war had begun King John died. His nine-year-old son Henry was his heir.

Because of the young age of King Henry III it was necessary that during his minority the responsibility of carrying on the government of England be entrusted to someone else. The king's council was faced with unusual circumstances in selecting who that person would be. Henry's mother was Isabel of Angouleme who was not English, but descended from French royalty; and England was at that time under papal authority. It was not deemed appropriate that either the queen or the pope's representative take over the governing of England. Before his death King John had recommended that his kingdom be put in the care of William Marshal, and the wisdom and leadership that William had consistently demonstrated made him the obvious choice of the council. In the fall of 1216 William Marshal was chosen to be the Regent of England and the protector of the young King Henry III. William was about seventy years old.

It was not an easy time to take over. England was in a state of disarray. The country was in the midst of a civil war, the treasury was empty, and much of the kingdom was in enemy hands. The strength of William's character and the esteem with which he was regarded by everyone enabled him to receive the cooperation of the papal representative and the ministers of the deceased king. With their support William set about the task of bringing the kingdom under control. For two and a half years William exercised his sound judgment, his military prowess, and his negotiating skills to successfully restore England to a position of strength and peace.

Many of the rebelling barons were easily persuaded to abandon their support of the French prince and join forces with the young King Henry III. Although they had been at war against King John, after his death they preferred to serve his son, an English born king, rather than the French monarch. Also, the problems which caused the barons to rebel were already being resolved under William's leadership. A revised version of the Magna Charta was issued, and William began to address the lack of funds by using jewels from the treasury and cloth from the royal wardrobe to make payments and settle debts. However, not all of the barons were immediately convinced to comply, and the civil war continued. William himself led the military forces that ultimately defeated the French and the barons who supported them, and the conditions of peace were established. Many of the opposing barons chose this time to leave the country temporarily and go on crusade to the Holy Land.

William used his power and negotiating skill to influence the princes and barons of Scotland, Wales, and Ireland to rejoin the kingdom and pay homage to the young King Henry III. In addition, judicial systems were established to resolve individual disputes and means of taxation were agreed upon. By the end of 1218 William had overseen the return of order and stability to the kingdom.

In February of 1219 William became ill and was confined to his bed. After several weeks, and realizing that he was dying, he asked that he be moved from the Tower of London where he had been residing to his manor in Caversham where he felt he would be more comfortable. During that period he had the presence of mind to make provisions for the continuation of care for the young king and to put his own personal affairs in order. Shortly before his death he called young King Henry III and various official representatives to his bedside. In front of witnesses he formally transferred responsibility for the king's welfare into the hands of the pope's representative. He provided for the security of his own wife and children by making his will. Also, he fulfilled a vow he had made on crusade by becoming a Knights Templar, and arranged to be buried at Temple Church in London.

William died on May 14, 1219. His funeral procession traveled slowly from his home in Caversham, to London, where his friend, Stephen Langton, the Archbishop of Canterbury, led his burial service. His body was laid to rest in the church of the Knights of the Temple in London.

Soon after William's death his son, "William the Younger," commissioned a biography to be written about his father. It is unknown who the author of the biography was, but it is evident that it was written by someone who knew him and his experiences well. It is because of that biography, *L'Histoire de Guillaume le Marechal,* that so much is known today about William the Marshal.

William the Marshal was mourned by all - kings, nobles, and ordinary men. Remarkable tributes were made to him by those who had fought beside him and those who had fought against him. He had lived a life that exemplified the finest virtues of his time. Those characteristics were recognized and admired by his contemporaries, and also earned him a renowned place in history. Even today, after many centuries have past, the reputation of William the Marshal as the paragon of knighthood remains intact.

3

David I, King of Scotland

David I of Scotland was another illustrious ancestor of Alice de Plumpton, and her 6th great-grandfather.

David I, King of Scotland

Henry of Scotland

William I, The Lion, King of Scotland

Isabella of Scotland

William de Ros

William de Ros

Lucy de Ros

William de Plumpton

Alice de Plumpton

David was a son of King Malcolm III and his second wife, Margaret. Malcolm III was the son of Duncan I and grandson of King Malcolm II of Scotland. After the death of Malcolm II in 1034, Duncan and his cousin MacBeth both claimed a right to the throne. Duncan succeeded to the throne but was later challenged and killed in battle by MacBeth. MacBeth then became king and ruled Scotland for seventeen years. After Duncan's death his young son Malcolm lived in exile while MacBeth prevailed in Scotland. However, Malcolm did not relinquish his right to the throne, and eventually Malcolm's forces defeated MacBeth in battle and Malcolm became king himself, ruling Scotland from 1058 until 1093.

Margaret, the daughter of Edward Atheling and his wife Agatha, was born in Hungary where her father, a nephew of Edward the Confessor, was living in exile. Edward the Confessor had no children, and Margaret's father was considered the likely heir to the English throne. The family was summoned to England, but Edward Atheling died soon after their arrival. Margaret and her mother, brother, and sister continued to live in England for several years, but sought refuge in Scotland after the death of Edward the Confessor and the invasion of William the Conqueror in 1066. Malcolm III welcomed the family into his court and, in fact, it was decided that Margaret would become his wife.

In 1070 Margaret and Malcolm III married. Their marriage combined two renowned royal lineages. Margaret's blood lines went back through Saxon kings, including Alfred the Great. Malcolm's lineage went back through the Scottish and Irish kings and on back through King David of Israel. The value they placed on these bloodlines is apparent in the names which were given to their children. Malcolm and Margaret had eight children, six sons and two daughters. Many of the sons were named for Saxon kings, and their youngest son was named David.

David was born in 1084. He spent his early childhood in Scotland, but by the time he was about ten years old both of his parents had died. His father, King Malcolm III, was killed while on a raid into England in 1093. His mother, Queen Margaret, died shortly after that. David's uncle claimed the Scottish throne after the death of Malcolm III, and a dangerous period followed when there were struggles for power between the sons of Malcolm III and their uncle. During this time David was sent to England. David's older sister, Edith (also known as Matilda), took care of her young brother. While David was still a teenager Matilda married Henry I, who had just become King of England. David, as a brother of the queen, became an important member of the English court. Meanwhile, David's older brother, Edgar, succeeded in seizing power from his uncle in Scotland. He ruled for ten years. When he died in 1097 his next younger brother Alexander succeeded him to the throne. However, Edgar's will designated that the Scottish lands be divided between Alexander and his other remaining brother, David. David became the ruler of the southern section of what is now Scotland, and he received the title of Earl of Cumbria.

His influence and power increased further when in 1113 he married Matilda of Huntingdon, the heiress of Waltheof, Earl of Northumbria. David and Matilda had one son, whom they named Henry. David's sister, Matilda, died in 1118, but David still retained the support of his brother-in-law, King Henry of England. When David's brother Alexander died in 1124 David, with Henry's powerful military backing, was able to prevail against the claims of his nephew (Alexander's son) to the Scottish throne. David's coronation took place that same year. David reigned as King of Scotland for almost thirty years. He is credited with bringing about significant social and political reforms in Scotland. David's close connection with the English royalty and his familiarity with English customs influenced the changes he initiated. He invited and gave properties in Scotland to many of his associates among the English nobility. He advanced the feudal system of western Europe into Scotland. This system included the creation of feudal lordships, the building of castles, the services of professional knights, and pledging homage.

This image depicts the obverse side of the Great Seal of David I, King of Scotland (Wikimedia Commons)

He increased his power and Scotland's influence through military maneuvers and the arrangement of strategic marriages, so that he ultimately dominated and controlled greater territory to the west and the north. After the death of Henry I of England in 1135 David supported Henry's daughter and only heir, Matilda, against Stephen. (Matilda was also David's niece.) When Stephen became king, David went to war against him, invading and occupying England several times over the next few years. Although David was not successful in obtaining the throne for Matilda he did acquire additional territory from northern England for Scotland. During David's reign Scotland's economy was revolutionized. David captured silver mines and a mint during his warring with King Stephen of England. As a result, silver mining increased the country's wealth and Scotland's first silver coins were minted. Also, David established royal burghs across Scotland. Burghs were towns which became centers of trade and government.

David expanded upon the religious innovations introduced into Scotland by his mother, Queen Margaret. He founded many monasteries and monastic orders. In addition to their religious impact, these monasteries furthered agricultural and administrative improvements.

David's only son, Henry, the Earl of Northumbria, married Ada de Warenne. They had three sons and three daughters who survived childhood. Henry died in 1152, before his father, and David quickly made arrangements that would assure that his successor would be Henry's oldest son. David died in 1153 and was succeeded by his eleven-year-old grandson, Malcolm IV of Scotland. Malcolm ruled for twelve years and then was succeeded by his brother, William I, The Lion.

During David's long sovereignty Scotland was transformed. The many reforms which David enacted spread the Norman influences that were already prevalent in England into Scotland. David I, King of Scotland was a pious and refined leader who oversaw the conversion of Scotland from a wild, barbarian territory into a civilized medieval nation.

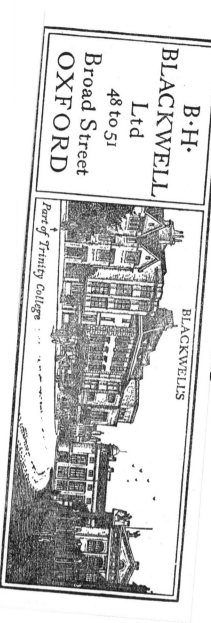

e Conqueror

Normandy, who became King William I of England, was
e of the major events in history, the Norman Conquest.
ngland and accession to the throne tied England to the
lted in the spread of European culture to the British Isles.
ueror was Alice de Plumpton's eighth great-grandfather.

William the Conqueror

Henry I

Matilda of England

Henry II

William Longespee

Ida Longespee

Maud de Beauchamp

Roger de Mowbray

John de Mowbray

Christiana de Mowbray

Alice de Plumpton

William was a direct descendant of Rollo, the founder of the Viking territory
that became known as Normandy. William's father was Robert who lived in
Falaise in Normandy and was the younger son of Richard II, Duke of
Normandy. One day Robert was returning to his family's castle when he
passed a group of peasant girls who were washing clothes in a stream. As the
barefooted girls were talking and laughing together, Robert's attention was
drawn to one of them, Herleve, and he was completely captivated. She was
the daughter of a humble tanner. Robert, being of noble birth, could not
consider marriage to a commoner. After returning to his castle, however, he
sent a messenger to Herleve's father requesting that she be permitted to

come to the castle to live with him. Herleve's father complied with the request, and Herleve and Robert lived together at the castle while remaining unmarried. They had a daughter, Adelaide, and a son, William.

William was born in 1028, shortly after his father had become Duke of Normandy. His early years were spent in the castle at Falaise. He enjoyed playing with the other children of the castle. His personal characteristics, as well as his father's title, made him a natural leader in their playful pursuits. William's father took great pride in his son; and because he was included in many of his father's activities, William became well-known and admired by the knights and nobles of Falaise. Robert determined that William would be his heir, and the next Duke of Normandy, even though he was illegitimate. When William was about seven years old, Robert decided to make a pilgrimage to the Holy Land. It would be a long and dangerous journey. As was customary, Robert needed to make arrangements for the governing of his lands while he was gone and to plan for the possibility that he might not survive the adventure. Since Robert was unmarried, there was some question as to who would be his successor should he not return from his pilgrimage. Robert had younger brothers and other relatives who had claims to the dukedom, and so he had to take steps to assure that his choice of an heir, William, would prevail. After the many preparations for the journey had been completed, Robert called a meeting of the noble men of his realm. When they had assembled Robert announced his plan to embark on a pilgrimage and designated William as his heir. He also appointed a governor to rule in his name while he was gone. Then Robert took William to King Henry of France. Robert and William both paid homage to the French king, and King Henry promised to care for William in his own court during Robert's absence. William's time in the French court served a dual purpose. It provided a safe haven for William, away from his challengers for the title of Duke of Normandy, and it also enabled the young boy to receive expert military training. Robert's provisions for his son turned out to be very critical, for Robert died during his journey back from Jerusalem in 1035.

The years following his father's death, during the time of his minority, were especially treacherous for William. The plans for governing that his father had arranged to be followed during his pilgrimage continued after his death, but were then done in William's name. However, his uncle and various other claimants to the dukedom challenged William's legitimacy as an heir. They assembled forces and made various attempts to seize control of Normandy.

His right to become duke and his life itself were in danger for over ten years, but the support structure that his father had established for him and William's own personal charisma and military bearing, even at a young age, enabled him to attract a strong following and to eventually prevail against the rebellions. His defeat of the rebelling Norman barons at the Battle of Val-des-Dunes near Caen in 1047, with the help of Henry I of France, finally assured his control of Normandy.

This did not end the necessity for his continued involvement in military actions, though. The following year he assisted Henry I in an attack against Geoffrey Martel, Count of Anjou. The townspeople of Alencon, in support of Geoffrey, taunted William and his men. They hung raw pelts ready for tanning from their buildings, in reference to William being the bastard child of Duke Robert and a tanner's daughter. William was greatly insulted, and when he succeeded in capturing the town he enacted cruel revenge.

Warfare was an ever-present aspect of a ruler's life, and access to men who would fight was critical to one's success. The feudal system, which had already existed in Normandy, was developed and further refined during William's rule. That means of governing enabled William to assemble powerful military support when he needed it. Basically, feudalism was an exchange of land for a promise of military support. Landowners in Normandy were vassals of William, their duke. These vassals were able to divide their land among knights who in turn would owe them allegiance in exchange for having land to live on and farm. At each level the tenants would pay homage to their immediate lords, with loyalty ultimately extending to their powerful duke. When military support was needed William had an abundant supply of fighters available from all levels. Thus, William's power as Duke of Normandy was enhanced by his country's means of governing.

In 1051 William visited Edward the Confessor in England. Edward had spent many years in exile in Normandy while England was occupied by the Danes. He had formed a close relationship with William because of his time spent in Normandy and also because he was a cousin of William's father. In 1042 Edward had ascended to the throne, and he had been ruling England for about ten years by the time of William's visit. Edward the Confessor had no established heirs, and William later asserted that Edward during this visit in 1051 had promised William that he would be his heir.

When William was about twenty-four he strengthened his position by marrying Matilda, who was the daughter of Baldwin V of Flanders and granddaughter of Robert II of France. Matilda was a direct descendant of King Alfred the Great of England. That line, through Matilda of Flanders, was one of the lines of descent for Alice de Plumpton from Alfred the Great.

Alfred the Great

Aelfthryth of Wessex

Arnulf I of Flanders

Baldwin III of Flanders

Arnulf II of Flanders

Baldwin IV of Flanders

Baldwin V of Flanders

Matilda of Flanders

Henry I

Matilda of England

Henry II

William Longespee

Ida Longespee

Maud de Beauchamp

Roger de Mowbray

John de Mowbray

Christiana de Mowbray

Alice de Plumpton

When William first requested that she marry him, she rejected him by saying, "Thou art mad, clown, to think that I, sprung from kings, will marry a bastard." She was convinced to marry him, however, when he forcefully grabbed her by her braids and flung her to the ground. Their marriage was opposed by the pope because William and Matilda were distantly related. They later founded two churches in Caen, St. Stephen's and Holy Trinity, as penance for marrying against the pope's wishes. As unpropitious a beginning as this would seem to be, they had a long marriage which produced several daughters and four sons, two of whom became kings of England.

Matilda of Flanders was the wife of William I of England. (Wikimedia Commons)

As William's status increased, his former patron, Henry I of France, began to feel threatened by the power of Normandy. He renounced his long alliance with William and joined forces with Geoffrey Martel of Anjou. Together they made two unsuccessful invasions of Normandy, one in 1054 and one in 1057; but both Henry I and Geoffrey later died in 1060, without having been able to check William's influence.

Two years later Harold Godwinson visited William in Normandy. Harold was the Earl of Wessex and also the brother-in-law of Edward the Confessor. During this visit in Normandy he made an oath to support William in his claim to succession to the English throne.

In January of 1066 Edward the Confessor died, childless. Despite William's belief that he had the commitment of Edward himself and the support of Harold in his claim to the English throne, it was Harold, and not William, who was made king. When William heard the news he began to make strategic preparations to enforce his own right to be King of England. He enlisted the support of his Norman barons, he obtained the neutrality of Henry I of Germany and Philip IV of France, he secured the blessing of the pope, and he formed a critical alliance with Tostig, the banished brother of Harold. William also arranged that his wife Matilda, with the assistance of appointed officers who would inform and advise her, would be in charge of the governing of Normandy during his absence.

At the same time, William assembled the men and ships that would be needed to invade England. His invasion force consisted of thousands of men, including infantry, cavalry, and archers. Those men were Normans, Flemish, and French. The accumulation of over six hundred ships to transport the troops across the English Channel, by acquiring available sea-worthy vessels and building and equipping new ones, was accomplished in about nine months time. One of the ships was a large vessel, elaborately decorated, which Matilda had arranged to be built as a parting gift for her husband.

On the Norman side of the English Channel the fleet assembled in early September at the mouth of a small river called the Dive which flowed from the area of the castle in Falaise to the Channel. Their departure was delayed for several weeks because of bad weather and unfavorable winds. Then on the 27th of September 1066 the Norman Invasion began. William and his men and fleet of ships left Normandy. They arrived in Pevensey on the southern coast of England the next day. They were able to land unchallenged, and to move along the Channel a few miles to the east to Hastings, where they set up their headquarters.

Although Harold and the English forces had been prepared for the possible invasion and had been guarding the southern coast of England, and the English Channel, with a large army and fleet of ships early in September, by the middle of September their numbers had dwindled, thinking that the Normans would not be invading as fall and winter weather approached. Then word had arrived that King Harald III of Norway and Tostig had joined together and invaded England to the north near York. Harold moved his forces northward to defend his realm, leaving the English Channel unguarded. He was successful in defeating the Viking invaders and was in the midst of celebrating his victory when he received word that William had landed and was situated at Hastings. In the beginning of October Harold marched his army south to London and prepared his defenses against the Norman invaders.

On October 13th William tried to negotiate a solution. He offered Harold three options to prevent the imminent battle. Harold could step down and give the throne to William, or he could let the pope decide the issue, or he could let the result be determined by a single combat. Harold declined all three. William then offered a compromise which would have allowed Harold and his brother to retain all of the English lands as territories under William's rule. Harold refused to give up his position as King of England, but offered to pay William any amount of money he demanded if he would abandon the invasion. William was unwilling to relinquish his claim to the throne. No compromise could be reached.

The next day the battle ensued. It was a hard-fought struggle between two strong forces. The opposing armies had about the same number of men, but William's troops included cavalry and many archers in addition to infantry. The English forces had only soldiers on foot and limited archers. At first the English forces were able to repel their attackers, and at one point it was rumored that William had been killed. He rode fully armored among his men and rallied them by lowering his helmet to reveal his face and assure them that he still lived. A break in the English line occurred when the Normans feigned retreat and the English broke their ranks to pursue them. That allowed the Norman cavalry to attack the English from behind. Also the archers began to aim high so that the unprotected faces of the enemy were hit. The battle lasted all day, and there were heavy casualties on both sides. By late afternoon Harold and his brothers were all dead, and the remaining Englishmen fled.

William was the victor. However, the English throne was not surrendered immediately to him. Instead, the young Edgar Atheling, the great-nephew of Edward the Confessor, was proclaimed king. William proceeded to march with his troops toward London, forcing Edgar to relinquish the crown. On Christmas Day 1066, he was crowned William I, King of England, in Westminster Abbey.

For several years following his coronation he faced English resistance to the Norman takeover. There were numerous revolts in various parts of England, and forces representing other claimants to the English throne attempted to seize control. William was able to defeat all of those adversaries. He faced his biggest challenge in northern England where the Northumbrians revolted in support of Edgar Atheling. Edgar's forces were joined by the army of Malcolm III of Scotland and a Danish fleet in an unsuccessful attempt to overthrow William. Their rebellion resulted in a severe punishment that became known as the "Harrying of the North." William ordered the burning and total destruction of the land to the extent that the area did not fully recover for over a century.

During the time in which William was consolidating his authority Matilda arrived in England and was crowned Queen of England; William's half-brother, Odo, was installed as the Earl of Kent; almost all of the land

William the Conqueror arrived in England in the fall of 1066 prior to the Battle of Hastings. (Wikimedia Commons)

previously owned by English nobility was redistributed to Norman warriors; and Englishmen were removed from most important religious and state positions and replaced by Normans. William traveled between England and Normandy overseeing the governing of both realms. By 1072 William had gained the acceptance and respect of his English subjects.

Around this time the Bayeux Tapestry was created to commemorate the Norman conquest. It was a series of linen panels which were embroidered with wool thread. The embroidery recorded the events surrounding the Battle of Hastings. William's half-brother, Odo, was the Bishop of Bayeux. The tapestry was first displayed when his cathedral at Bayeux was dedicated in 1077. There is a legend that Matilda did the embroidery to honor her husband's campaign. However, most authorities now feel that it was commissioned by Bishop Odo and embroidered by skilled English needle workers. The Bayeux Tapestry still exists as a part of the historical record and evidence of the tribute paid to William the Conqueror.

The Norman Invasion, and William's subsequent reign greatly changed England. Large numbers of Normans began to populate England, bringing their language and customs with them. French became the official language of the royalty and the courts of England. The feudal system of Normandy spread to England. That resulted in the erection of numerous Norman castles scattered throughout the land. One of the most famous of those was the White Tower, the stone structure that would later be expanded to become the Tower of London. It was begun in 1078. William diminished the power of the earls in England. As old earldoms lapsed, the English earls were replaced by Normans who were limited to single shires. The English system of governing, with sheriffs and courts, was retained and strengthened. William, himself, was very involved in the administration of the various parts of his kingdom. He ordered a survey of all landowners and their assets in order to learn about his realm and be able to tax more efficiently. The record of that survey, which was completed in 1086, became known as the *Domesday Book* and still exists as a valuable reference. William was successful in realigning the organization and population of England in a way that lessened the probability of successful rebellions and facilitated his control.

Invading England, establishing control and the necessary reorganization there, and then ruling both his duchy and his kingdom required William's concentrated effort and active involvement. In addition, during those years

(Wikimedia Commons)

he had personal family issues with which he had to deal. His second son, Richard, died in a hunting accident. Two of his daughters also died. Marriages were arranged for several of his daughters. His oldest son, Robert, rebelled against his father and tried repeatedly, but unsuccessfully, to gain control of Normandy. William's half-brother, Odo, eventually caused problems in his position in England and was imprisoned. In 1083 Matilda, William's wife of over thirty years, died.

This map shows the dominions of William the Conqueror about 1087. (Wikimedia Commons)

William's involvement in warfare continued throughout the later years of his life. His final military operation was an invasion into France in 1087 which William undertook in retaliation for raids that had been made into Normandy. His forces assaulted and burned the town of Mantes. As William rode through the town surveying the smoldering ruins his horse suddenly lurched as its foot hit a burning ember. William was thrown forward with great force against the pommel of his saddle. He was able to keep from falling from his horse, but sustained a serious internal injury. In great pain, William was conveyed to Rouen in Normandy.

He was attended by physicians and bishops and monks for several weeks, but his condition worsened. Realizing that he was about to die, William sought forgiveness for the harsh ways in which he had dealt with some of those who had opposed him. Having always been a pious man, he arranged for most of his wealth to be distributed to the poor and to the church. He also expressed his wishes in regard to his three sons. He directed that his son Robert be given the dukedom of Normandy as he had promised years earlier, even though Robert was still in conflict with his father and not present at his death. He expressed his desire that William Rufus succeed him as King of England, and that Henry be given five thousand pounds in silver.

On September 9th 1087, William died. His body was taken to Caen, Normandy for burial. His funeral was disrupted by several irregularities. The service was interrupted by a fire in the town, and most of the participants needed to leave to assist in fighting the fire. Also, it was discovered that the stone coffin was not large enough for the body, since William had become extremely overweight when he was older. The monks conducting the service had to force the body into the casket. In addition, as they prepared to bury the body the original owner of the land where he was being buried demanded that he be compensated for the property since it had been taken unjustly by the duke years earlier. Finally, however, William was buried in Caen at St. Stephen's, one of the two churches which he and Matilda had founded at the time of their marriage. Matilda had been buried at the other church, Holy Trinity, four years earlier.

William the Conqueror was Duke of Normandy for fifty-two years and King of England for twenty-one years. He was the first Norman king of England and was responsible for spreading the culture and customs of Europe into England. All of the English monarchs since the eleventh century have been his direct descendents. William the Conqueror was one of the most powerful men of his time and one of the most influential men in history.

5

Rollo the Viking

During the early Middle Ages adventurers from the northern lands that are now Scandinavian countries traveled by boat and raided neighboring areas, surviving on the spoils of their attacks. Those seafarers were called Vikings. One of their leaders was Rollo. He was the thirteenth great-grandfather of Alice de Plumpton.

Rollo

William I

Richard I

Richard II

Robert I

William I of England (William the Conqueror)

Henry I

Matilda of England

Henry II

William Longspee

Ida Longspee

Maud de Beauchamp

Roger de Mowbray

John de Mowbray

Christiana de Mowbray

Alice de Plumpton

Rolf, Hrolfr, and Rouf are different names that refer to Rollo. He was also sometimes called Rollo the Walker, because he was very large and his great size made it difficult for him to find a horse he could ride comfortably. Rollo was born in the middle of the ninth century. Details about his early life are unclear. There is disagreement among historians as to his country of origin and his parentage, but the most prevalent view is that Rollo was born into a family of chieftains in Norway as the son of Earl Ragnvald and his wife Hild. Earl Ragnvald was a relative and advisor to Harold, the first king of Norway. Despite his parents' close connection to the king, Rollo was banished from Norway because he was caught plundering within his own land. The Viking chieftains earned their livelihoods by raiding other settlements, and their exploits were accepted and even admired by their contemporaries. However, King Harold had forbidden his subjects to loot from their own countrymen, and although Rollo's mother interceded on his behalf King Harold insisted that Rollo could no longer remain in Norway.

Actually, banishment would not have been that different than the life with which Rollo was familiar. He was accustomed to sailing away with his companions for long periods of time. So having been told to leave Norway, he set sail with other wild and adventurous young men who chose to follow him, and they sought different lands to plunder.

This primitive painting from the 14ᵗʰ century shows Rollo and the Vikings. (Wikimedia Commons)

He and the other Vikings used wooden boats that were narrow, with the front and back ends being symmetrical. They were often carved to look like dragons. The ships each had one sail, but they depended on rowing for their speed and maneuverability. They had twelve to sixteen rowing benches, with oarsmen at both ends of each bench. Rollo assembled a fleet of those boats to carry his band of men as they traveled on the northern rivers and seas.

Rollo and his followers explored the rugged and desolate islands off the northwest coast of Scotland where they discovered other adventurers who wished to join them. They added to their fleet of ships and supply of arms and munitions of war. Then they sailed south along the coasts of Scotland and England. Their raids of the English coasts were largely unsuccessful because Alfred the Great, the English monarch at that time, had strongly fortified his shores against such incursions. Seeking easier areas to plunder they worked their way through the Straits of Dover and began assaults on Flanders. During one battle the Vikings captured the Count of Hainault. Rollo offered to release him to his wife for a large ransom. The countess was able to procure the necessary funds, and the count was set free. By means of activities such as that Rollo was able to finance his exploits and also to add to his already fearsome reputation.

When Rollo was still a young chieftain in 885, he joined other Viking leaders in an assault on Paris. Their combined fleets contained several hundred ships as they besieged the city. The citizens of Paris were able to withstand the attack and prevent the Vikings from entering their highly fortified city, but that did not stop the Vikings from continuing their raids in that area for many years. Sometimes the Franks would resist the attacks and engage in battle. Other times they would pay the marauders in order to avoid the heavy losses that would result from combat.

Some years later Rollo traveled along the Seine River and made camp near the city of Rouen. The inhabitants of the city knew that they were ill-prepared to resist attack themselves and that their king and his forces were not in the area to protect them. An archbishop from the city was courageous enough to go to Rollo's camp to try to negotiate a peaceful settlement. Rollo promised that if he and his men could peacefully take over the city they would not harm anyone inhabiting it, and that is what was accomplished. After settling in, Rollo fortified Rouen and established it as his headquarters.

The King of France at that time was Charles III, who was called Charles the Simple. King Charles fought Rollo for many years, as Rollo attempted to enlarge his territory in France. Rollo, already having a strong base in Rouen, was able to prevail in most of the battles of their protracted war, and with each victory Rollo gained both territory and prestige. He established means of governing his conquered subjects, and grew adept as a ruler who was fair and also able to maintain order. Finally, King Charles was forced to negotiate a settlement with Rollo. In 911 it was arranged that Rollo would be given the vast expanse of land which now constitutes Normandy, but it would continue to be a part of the realm of King Charles. Rollo would govern the inhabitants of his territory, but he and his subjects would all promise their fealty to the King of France. Monetary tribute and military support would be a part of that fealty. The arrangement that they negotiated resulted in the governmental organization that would later be called the Duchy of Normandy.

This Rollo monument is in Alesund, Norway. (Wikimedia Commons)

In addition to Rollo's pledge of allegiance to the king, the treaty specified that King Charles' daughter Giselle would become Rollo's wife, and that Rollo must become a Christian. Three official ceremonies were necessary in order for those things to be accomplished. The first of those was the act of homage, which was a ritual of public submission to one's master. As a part of the ceremony Rollo was required by French tradition to kiss the king's foot as he knelt in front of him. Rollo would not consent to that aspect of the ritual. After some discussion a compromise was reached when Rollo ordered one of his attendants to kiss the foot of the king. The reluctant attendant obeyed Rollo, but in the process of complying he lifted the foot of the king so abruptly that King Charles lost his balance and tumbled to the ground. Having promised fealty to King Charles, Rollo was then baptized at the cathedral in Rouen. He was given the Christian name Robert. Following his baptism he and Giselle were married.

ROLLO, Konung der Noormannen.
(Wikimedia Commons)

Rollo's final years were spent as a respected and effective ruler. Although he had spent most of his life as a wild warrior who survived from the results of his plundering and had no permanent home, he was very successful in adjusting to the requirements of governing his own realm. He ruled wisely and fairly. The land he had acquired was greatly improved under his direction and became one of the most prosperous regions in Europe. Criminal behavior was severely punished, and his realm was exceedingly peaceful. A famous story related that one day Rollo was out hunting with his companions and decided to demonstrate how safe his land was and how honest his subjects were. He took off two gold bracelets he had been wearing and hung them from a tree branch, clearly visible from the road. When he and his associates traveled by a few weeks later the bracelets were still hanging there, and he was able to retrieve them.

Although many Vikings had settled with Rollo the original inhabitants also remained and continued to farm the land. The territory which Rollo ruled later became known as Normandy because so many of its inhabitants were the descendants of Rollo and his fellow Vikings, the men from the North.

Rollo and Giselle had no children. However, Rollo already had children at the time of his marriage to Giselle. One of those children was William, who was known as William Longsword. William's mother was Poppa. About four years before he died, Rollo passed the governance of his land on to his son William, who became William I of Normandy. Rollo died around 931 and was buried at the cathedral in Rouen.

This effigy of Rollo of Normandy is in the cathedral in Rouen. (Wikimedia Commons)

Rollo, the Viking, was the first leader of what became known as Normandy. In his early life he was renowned as a wild seafarer, a courageous chieftain, and a strong warrior. In his later life he became highly-regarded as a wise and just ruler. Rollo had many famous descendants who inherited his combination of adventurous Viking traits and leadership qualities.

6

Alfred the Great

Alfred the Great is known as the maker of England. Living during the ninth century, he became the epitome of what a king should be. He earned renown for his military leadership, his strengthening of the church, his development of an effective legal system, and his advancement of learning. Alfred the Great was the fourteenth great-grandfather of Alice de Plumpton.

Alfred the Great

Edward the Elder

Edmund I

Edgar

Ethelred II

Edmund II

Edward the Exile

Margaret Atheling

David I, King of Scotland

Henry of Scotland

William I, The Lion, King of Scotland

Isabella of Scotland

William de Ros

William de Ros

Lucy de Ros

William de Plumpton

Alice de Plumpton

In the middle of the ninth century the area that is now present day England consisted of four separate kingdoms – Northumberland, Mercia, East Anglia, and Wessex. Alfred was born in 848 at the royal palace at Wantage in

Wessex. He was the youngest son of Ethelwulf, the king of Wessex, and his first wife, Osburga. Alfred had three older brothers and one sister. He was a handsome child with a pleasing disposition, and was a favorite of his parents. He was also very intelligent. It is said that when he was still quite young his mother showed a beautifully illustrated book to her sons and told them that whichever one of them could learn how to read it first would be given the book. Alfred was highly motivated and, although he was the youngest, he acquired the book. Whether he learned to read or had memorized the poetic contents is unclear.

Queen Osburga is pictured with her son, Alfred. (Wikimedia Commons)

When Alfred was just five years old he was sent with a royal entourage to visit Rome. While there, he was confirmed by Pope Leo IV and was anointed as a future king. Two years later he again traveled to Rome, this time accompanying his father. They remained in Rome for about a year, and Alfred received religious instruction. Ethelwulf, himself, had been brought up in a monastery, so it would have been important to him to expose Alfred to religious training. Their trip to Rome involved much pomp and splendor.

Ethelwulf presented gifts to the dignitaries in Rome and financed the rebuilding of a seminary there.

En route to Rome they visited the king of France, Charles the Bald. Alfred's mother had died when he was very young, and after returning from Rome Ethelwulf married his second wife, Judith, the daughter of the king of France. Judith was much younger than Ethelwulf, and just a few years older than Alfred.

While Ethelwulf and Alfred had been in Rome Alfred's older brothers had managed things at home. After their return his oldest brother Ethelbald was reluctant to relinquish his power and threatened a rebellion, so he was installed as ruler of part of the realm as a compromise. Just two years later, in 858, Ethelwulf died. Ethelbald became king of all of Wessex when his father died. He also married his father's widow, the young Judith. Ethelbald's reign lasted only two years, until he died. He was succeeded by another brother, Ethelberht, who ruled for about five years, until his death. A third brother, Ethelred, ascended the throne in 866. It was during Ethelred's reign that Alfred began to play an active public role.

During this time in history the kingdoms that comprised Britain were experiencing almost constant threats of Viking attacks. What had been raids into their territories had become invasions with intent to conquer. The kingdoms that surrounded Wessex were gradually coming under the control of the Danes. During Ethelred's reign Alfred was acknowledged as the successor to the throne, and together the two brothers fought to defend their land from the Danes.

In 868 Alfred married Ealhswith, whose mother was a member of the Mercian royal family. Mercia was the region adjoining Wessex. At that time the Vikings were making many assaults on Mercia, and Alfred and his brother assisted unsuccessfully in its defense. When the attacks spread into Wessex Alfred helped his brother in attempting to resist the Viking incursions into their land. They engaged in numerous battles with mixed results. During an especially difficult year, which began towards the end of 870, there were nine major engagements with the Danes.

In the spring of 871 Ethelred died, and after that Alfred was in full charge of defending their territory. An uneasy peace was accomplished for several years through the payment of tribute, and the Danes occupied themselves with invasions in other regions. Of the four kingdoms Wessex was the only one remaining independent and not in the power of the Danes. However, by 876 they had returned, led by the Danish king Guthrum. Early in 878 they surprised and routed King Alfred and his companions at the royal castle. Many of them were killed, but Alfred and a few of his followers escaped and fled into the nearby forests and swamps. For several months Alfred existed in disguise as he covertly gathered forces and made plans to defeat the enemy. It is said that during this period he kept his identity secret as he sought shelter among his subjects, and that he was in one instance chastised by a farm wife for letting the cakes burn when he had been instructed to watch them. During this same period Alfred is said to have disguised himself as a blind harpist in order to gain entry into his enemy's camp. While entertaining Guthrum and his men he was able to determine their resources. Alfred finalized his preparations for facing the Danes and in the spring, joined by other forces in the region, he met the Danes in battle at Wiltshire. It was a decisive victory for Alfred, and the Danish king Guthrum and many of his chiefs converted to Christianity as a part of their peace agreement in 878, an agreement which became known as the peace of Wedmore. Guthrum and his followers settled in an area near Wessex and supported Alfred against other Danish invasions. This was a turning point in Alfred's battles with the Danes.

The Vikings partially deserted the British Isles for several years and concentrated their attacks on the continent. It was generally a peaceful time for Britain, but there still were occasional incursions. Alfred was able to expand his territory to include the city of London as a result of successfully repressing a Danish revolt in 885. Then, in 892 a prolonged campaign against Wessex began. The Danes invaded with more than three hundred ships, which were divided into two forces. The fighting to repel the invaders continued for four years, but Alfred's military power, both on land and water, prevailed. The Danes finally abandoned the battle and withdrew. Wessex remained independent. Alfred reinforced his position of power by arranging the marriage of his daughter to the ruler of Mercia, and thereby securing Mercia as a part of his realm.

Alfred is highly regarded for his military leadership and his success in ridding Britain of the Viking threat. He was able to achieve his victories because of the confidence he inspired in his followers and because of the military reforms he initiated. He learned from his early difficulties in repelling the Viking attacks. He analyzed what his military's weaknesses were in the battles with the Danes and sought to overcome those deficiencies. His improvements included the enforcement of the obligation of large landowners to provide fighting troops to assist in the country's defense, the division of the military troops into two groups which would alternate active service, and the establishment of a series of fortifications and garrisons for the troops located strategically across the realm. He also increased the emphasis placed on the navy, having ships built according to his own design. That his improvements were worth the huge investment in manpower and money is evidenced by his ultimate victories. As impressive as King Alfred's success was in military matters, however, that is just one of his areas of greatness.

Alfred was fond of reading and learning. (Wikimedia Commons)

Another one of Alfred's major contributions was the restoration of the dignity of the Church. He was a devout Christian, who had visited the pope in Rome twice as a child. When the pagan Danes attacked the territories within Britain they looted and ruined many monasteries and churches. In addition to supporting the rebuilding of the religious institutions that had already existed, Alfred founded some new monasteries. He also encouraged the conversion of the defeated Danes to Christianity.

King Alfred is regarded as England's greatest king. (Wikimedia Commons)

The destruction of the religious institutions had impacted the educational development of the people, as well as their religious well-being, since the monasteries were the centers of learning. Alfred had an intense lifelong interest in learning and education. He contributed to the advancement of learning through his own personal example and through his promotion of education for others. The years of Danish incursions had destroyed both the desire and the opportunity for learning. Albert determined to remedy both. He established a school at his court to which he invited scholars from other countries. Those scholars and Alfred himself translated several volumes of philosophical and religious text from Latin into what we now call Old English, so that his subjects could understand them. Some of Alfred's translations included his own personal observations and original writings. He also directed the writing of *The Anglo-Saxon Chronicle,* a chronological history of the times. That manuscript was copied and updated by various monasteries, and several versions still exist today as valuable sources of information about events in the early Middle Ages.

Still another aspect of Alfred's greatness was the code of law which he enacted. Alfred's *Doom Book* was a collection of the law codes of three Saxon Christian kingdoms (Wessex, Mercia, and Kent) to which he incorporated the Mosaic laws. The resulting code of law was a very detailed and Biblical-based system which eventually evolved into English common law. Alfred took a very active role in ensuring that justice be administered fairly and evenly, to rich and poor alike.

King Alfred died in 899. His life had been filled with accomplishment. The successes he experienced and the decisions he made impacted history tremendously. He demonstrated to future generations what the ideal king could be – powerful, intelligent, devout, just, and devoted to the best interests of his subjects. Alfred and his wife, Ealhswith, had two sons and three daughters. Their eldest son, Edward the Elder, succeeded his father to the throne. Included in Alfred's translation of Boethius' *Consolation of Philosophy* is this sentence: "My will was to live worthily as long as I lived, and after my life to leave to them that should come after, my memory in good works." Alfred succeeded completely in fulfilling his stated wish. He is remembered now, over twelve hundred years after his death, as Alfred the Great. A plaque stands in his hometown of Wantage, Oxfordshire, England bearing the following inscription:

"ALFRED THE GREAT

THE WEST SAXON KING.
BORN AT WANTAGE A.D. 849.

———————

ALFRED FOUND LEARNING DEAD,
AND HE RESTORED IT.
EDUCATION NEGLECTED
AND HE REVIVED IT.
THE LAWS POWERLESS
AND HE GAVE THEM FORCE.
THE CHURCH DEBASED
AND HE RAISED IT.
THE LAND RAVAGED BY A FEARFUL ENEMY,
FROM WHICH HE DELIVERED IT.

———————

ALFRED'S NAME WILL LIVE AS LONG
AS MANKIND SHALL RESPECT THE PAST."

7

Charlemagne

Charlemagne, the Emperor of the West, was the ruler of the Frankish people who inhabited what is now Germany and France. During his long reign, which began in the middle of the eighth century, he expanded the realm he had inherited from his father and succeeded in unifying most of Europe under one ruler for the first time since the Roman Empire. Charlemagne was the seventeenth great-grandfather of Alice de Plumpton.

Charlemagne

Pippin

Bernard

Pippin

Herbert I

Herbert II

Albert I

Herbert III

Otho

Herbert IV

Adelaide de Vermandois

Isabel de Vermandois

Ada de Warenne

William I, The Lion, King of Scotland

Isabella of Scotland

William de Ros

William de Ros

Lucy de Ros

William de Plumpton

Alice de Plumpton

Records existing during the lifetime of Charlemagne referred to him as *Carolus*. The name Charlemagne, which is the French translation for the Latin name *Carolus Magnus*, was added in later histories to distinguish him from his grandfather and son who were also named *Carolus*. The English translation of *Carolus Magnus* is Charles the Great. A prominent source of information about Charles is a biography, *Vita Karoli Magni,* written by Eginhard in the early ninth century. Eginhard was a minister of public works, councilor, and personal secretary of Charles. Much of the knowledge we have today about Charles' life, his accomplishments, and life in his court traces back to Eginhard's original writings.

Charles was born in 742, the son of Pippin the Short and his wife Bertrada. Charles' paternal grandfather was Charles Martel, the mayor of the palace (the governmental and military leader) of the Franks in the early eighth century. The Merovingian dynasty had for hundreds of years been the official line of kings who reigned over the Franks, but by the time of Charles Martel they were merely ceremonial figures, and the real power rested with the mayors of the palace. After Charles Martel's death his two sons, Pippin and Carloman, shared the responsibilities of the powerful position of mayor of the palace. Carloman chose after a few years to abandon his position and enter a monastery, and Pippin became the sole mayor of the palace. During Pippin's rule the Merovingian line of kings was formally deposed, and the Carolingian line founded by Charles Martel officially took over. Pippin was crowned King of the Franks by the pope in 754; and his two sons, Charles and Carloman, were anointed and designated as future kings at that time.

As a young man growing up in the Frankish court Charles had little exposure to formal learning, but become very adept in the use of weapons. He was also tall, strong, and healthy. He assisted his father, Pippin, in battle while still a teenager and was placed in charge of governing several counties in 763.

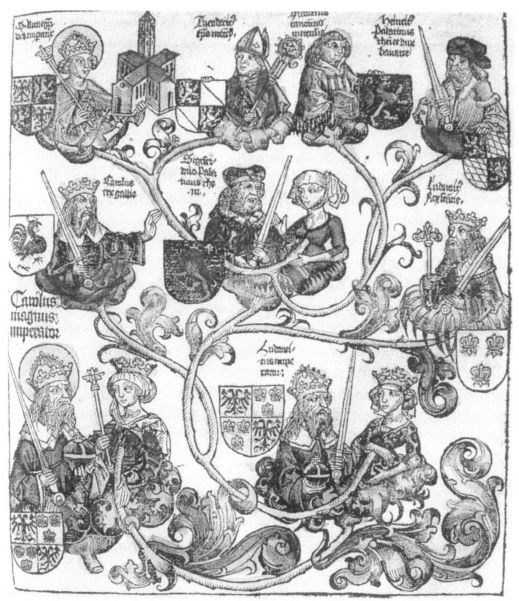

This pictorial family tree portrays the genealogy of Charlemagne. (Wikimedia Commons)

Pippin divided his realm between his two sons in 768, and when he died later that year Charles became the ruler of the northern portion of the Frankish kingdom and his brother Carloman became the ruler of the territory his uncle had previously ruled. About that same time Charles' mother, Bertrada, negotiated with Desiderius, the king of the Lombards who inhabited what is now northern Italy. She arranged a marriage between Charles and the king's daughter, in an attempt to secure peaceful relations between the Franks and the Lombards. Her plan was unsuccessful, though, because Charles repudiated the marriage several months after the wedding, and his wife returned to her father.

Charles and his brother, Carloman, did not get along well. When Charles requested Carloman's assistance in suppressing a rebellion in Aquitaine shortly after he became ruler his brother did not supply that help. Charles was able to successfully defeat his enemy without his brother's assistance, however. Hunold of Aquitaine fled to Gascony to seek safety, but ultimately the Duke of Gascony surrendered Hunold and also submitted himself to Charles. Quickly Charles' authority and territory were increasing. About three years later Carloman died. His widow and two small sons fled to seek refuge with Desiderius the king of the Lombards. Charles became the sole ruler of the Franks.

He then had the undivided power of the entire Frankish kingdom behind him, a power which continued to increase under his leadership. During his entire reign Charles was engaged in wars of conquest. Warfare was an accepted way of life for the Frankish people of that time, and the warriors viewed battle as their normal occupation, not just an occasional interruption to their lives. Charles' military genius enabled him to organize his warriors and carry out multiple campaigns simultaneously and over extended periods of time. Early in his reign he undertook his first Saxon campaign, a struggle which would continue for over thirty years. During those years he was involved in numerous other major battles which resulted in additions to his kingdom and his authority.

One area where military effort was expended was in Italy where the Lombards dwelled. In 773 Charles traveled over the Alps to Rome to defend the pope, Hadrian I. He defeated Desiderius, the king of the Lombards, after a long siege. Desiderius was sent into a monastery, and Charles was given the titles of "King of the Lombards" and "Patrician of the Romans."

In 777 he was lured into Spain to assist the Saracens, with the promise of additional cities being added to his realm. Although he was successful in extending his territory, when returning from Spain his forces were ambushed in a pass going through the Pyrenees, and his rearguard was almost completely destroyed. This disaster which happened in 778 is recognized as Charles' greatest defeat and was immortalized in legendary form by the *Chanson de Roland*, an epic poem which is the oldest surviving example of French literature.

Albrecht Durer painted this portrait of Charlemagne in 1512. (Wikimedia Commons)

Over the years Charles consolidated his authority in Italy where he installed Frankish counts in various areas. He used his power to protect and defend the pope and the church's holdings. In 795 Leo III became pope, and several years later he called upon Charles to defend him against attacks. Leo became the first pope to overtly recognize Charles as sovereign of Rome. Charles traveled to Rome in 800 and was crowned Emperor and *Augustus* by Leo III. This established King Charles as the Holy Roman Emperor.

The Saxons inhabited the land on the eastern frontiers of the Frankish kingdom. They had not been exposed to the earlier Roman invasions and remained untouched by some of the elements of culture that had been introduced to the Franks. Charles' battles with the Saxons were the most enduring and intense of his military struggles, and resulted in brutality and great loss of life on both sides. Charles insisted that all those defeated must denounce pagan ways, accept Christianity, and unite as one people under Frankish rule. He would subdue an uprising with assurances that the enemy had submitted, only to find after a short time that those conquered had reverted to their previous practices. This was perhaps because all Saxony was not united under one ruler. The submission of one faction did not mean that all Saxons had been subdued. Many of the Saxons did unite behind a patriot and rebel named Witikind for a number of years. He would lead uprisings and then flee with his Saxon fighters into the northern Danish territory. Eventually Witikind submitted to Charles and accepted baptism. Priests and monks traveled with the armies and were present to perform baptisms as those conquered accepted Christianity. Having reduced an area of Saxony to dependency Charles would assume responsibility for its protection. This would result in additional battles, as well as further extension of Frankish rule. Charles' ultimate success was partly a result of his ability to incorporate those conquered into his own fighting forces. Eventually, after thirty-two years of warring, the Saxons were completely subdued. Thousands of those who had resisted were relocated with their families to other parts of the kingdom. By 804 Saxony had been completely integrated into Charles' empire.

In addition to the campaigns against the Lombards and the Saxons, which continued for so many years, Charles engaged in numerous other battles, often simultaneously. He subdued the Bretons, the Bavarians, the Slavs, the Huns, the Danes, and the wild tribes that existed at that time. By the end of his reign the Frankish kingdom had been enlarged to be three times the size it had been when he first began to rule, and it extended over most of Europe.

Charles' military accomplishments, which resulted from years of involvement in brutal battle, are just a part of what earned him the name Charles the Great. He did unite almost all of Europe for the first time since the Roman Empire. By joining those diverse peoples under one ruler and under one religion, Christianity, he forged common institutions and bonds that would continue to unite them when they were later to be divided again into separate countries and governments. But his success in expanding his kingdom was only one aspect of his greatness.

He was a devout Christian and his religious policies strengthened, and regulated, the influence of the church. In addition to spreading Christianity through his conquests and being the protector of the pope, Charles oversaw the activities of the church and personally wielded much power in deciding religious matters.. Charles contributed liberally to the church in Rome. He also built churches and monasteries throughout his kingdom. He built a beautiful basilica at Aix-la-Chapelle, near his favorite palace. He adorned that church with silver, brass, and gold vessels and lamps. He imported columns and marble to decorate it. Charles worshipped there regularly and took an active interest in assuring that all religious ceremonies were conducted properly. Charles' devoutness as a Christian included caring for the poor. He donated to those in need within his kingdom, and also contributed to poor Christians in other countries.

Charles had an intense interest in learning. In spite of the time and effort devoted to battle and the fact that he lived during an era, and in a place, that had been devoid of scholarship, Charles advanced an appreciation of the importance of education. He set up a school within his palace to which he invited foreign scholars. He involved his own family in educational pursuits, and he himself became a very avid learner. He learned to read in both his native language and in Latin, and enjoyed reading to learn about diverse subjects, such as history and science and religion. He questioned visitors from foreign nations in order to learn about other parts of the world. He established schools throughout his kingdom, devoted to the education of both clergy and laymen.

Another aspect of Charles' greatness was his administrative ability. His exceptional organizational skills and intellectual energy enabled him to determine needs, devise solutions, and execute his plans with attention to detail in all facets of his kingdom's operation. In addition to directing the military conquests and managing church matters, he organized the means of governing his vast realm effectively. He organized his empire into counties, which were districts headed by counts. He utilized a system of required military service of all freemen and property holders, which supplied a steady fighting force. He established a system of officials which enabled him to involve public participation at assemblies where local concerns were addressed. He was able to attend to agricultural, commercial, financial, educational, and all of the other matters that were necessary for the prosperity of his vast realm. He organized the laws already existing in the various parts of his realm and added to them, creating a uniform system of laws that promoted the Christian principles he espoused. He also developed very successful and amicable relationships with foreign powers. His power and authority enabled him to form alliances, which added to the prosperity of his kingdom. He appears to have been able, by means of balancing the necessity of delegating some matters and applying personal detailed attention to others, to bring about the smooth administration of his entire realm.

Charles was a powerful and extremely busy ruler, but he was also devoted to his family. He had four wives. His first marriage was to the daughter of Desiderius. It was arranged by his mother, and he repudiated it after a short time. They had no children. Very soon afterwards in 771 he married Hildegarde, a princess of the Alamanni. They had nine children. After Hildegards's death he married Fastrada, with whom he had two children. His fourth wife was Luitgard, with whom he had no children. Charles had several concubines who also bore him children. Altogether Charles had twenty known children. He delighted in their company and took them with him on his journeys. His sons would ride on horseback beside him and his daughters would ride behind them with bodyguards. He dined with his children regularly and studied beside his sons and daughters at the palace school. In addition to their academic learning he directed that his sons be taught horsemanship and the practice of war and the chase. He made sure that his daughters learned cloth-making and other feminine skills. Charles was not willing to have his daughters marry, but several of them had children. He welcomed all of his grandchildren and enjoyed their presence at the palace. Charles also had a close relationship with his mother, and she lived at the palace with them until her death.

This map shows Europe at the time of the death of Charles the Great in 814.   (Wikimedia Commons)

This engraving of Charlemagne dates from the end of the sixteenth century. (Wikimedia Commons)

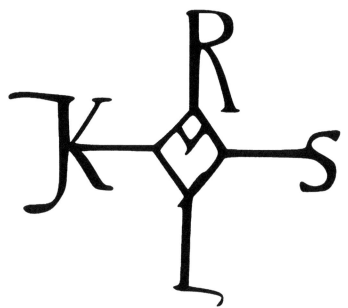

This monogram was used by Charlemagne on 31 August 790. (Wikimedia Commons)

As Charles grew older he entrusted more of his military campaigns to his sons and no longer led his armies. In 806 he divided his dominions between his three legitimate sons, Charles, Pippin, and Louis. However, his son Pippin died in 810 and his son Charles died in 811. Charles then named Louis as his successor; and in September of 813 at a ceremony at Aix, in the presence of the chief men of the kingdom of the Franks, Louis was crowned Emperor and *Augustus* to rule with his father.

Charles enjoyed good health for most of his life. He believed in moderation in food and drink, and he had a very active life style. In addition to the energy expended in carrying out and always expanding the duties of his position, he engaged in hunting and swimming for sport. Although slowed somewhat by old age and limping because of rheumatism, Charles continued his activities. Following the crowning of Louis he went hunting for several weeks. He returned to his palace as winter set in, and in January he was overcome by fever. He went to bed and, ignoring the advice of his physicians, he followed his normal procedure of abstaining from food to starve the fever. His condition was complicated by pleurisy. Seven days after taking to his bed, Charles died on the 28th of January, 814.

Charles had previously made a will which left most of his possessions to the churches within his realm, and the remainder to his children, his servants, and the poor. His will did not include instructions for his burial, but it was decided that the appropriate place to entomb him was in the basilica he had erected and adorned near the palace. He was buried there the same day he died. A golden arch was built above the tomb which bore his image and an inscription. The inscription stated in part:

> "In this tomb lies the body of Charles, the Great and Orthodox Emperor, who gloriously extended the kingdom of the Franks and reigned prosperously for forty-seven years."

8

Charles Martel

Charles Martel was mayor of the palace in the kingdom of the Franks during the eighth century. He is best known for being victorious in the Battle of Tours and, therefore, stopping the Arab invasion of Europe. He was the nineteenth great-grandfather of Alice de Plumpton.

Charles Martel

Pippin

Charlemagne

Pippin

Bernard

Pippin

Herbert I

Herbert II

Albert I

Herbert III

Otho

Herbert IV

Adelaide de Vermandois

Isabel de Vermandois

Ada de Warenne

William I, The Lion, King of Scotland

Isabella of Scotland

William de Ros

William de Ros

Lucy de Ros

William de Plumpton

Alice de Plumpton

Charles Martel was born about 688. He was the son of Pippin II, who was also known as Pippin of Heristal, and his concubine, Chalpaida. Pippin II was the mayor of the palace of the three Frankish kingdoms - Austrasia, Neustria, and Burgundy. The Franks were Germanic tribes who were united under the Merovingian kings in the late fifth century. Over the years the Merovingians had become powerless kings who were merely figureheads. The power of governing rested in the office of mayor of the palace. It was that position of authority that Charles' father held.

Pippin had a wife named Plectrude. He and Plectrude had two sons, Drogo and Grimwald, whom Pippin had placed in the mayoral positions in Neustria and Burgundy, while he retained his position in Austrasia. Both sons died before their father, but when Pippen died in 714, his widow claimed that Grimwald's young son was his rightful successor. She had Charles put into prison to thwart any effort he might make to claim his right to his father's position. At that same time a civil war broke out within the Frankish kingdoms. The nobles in Neustria rebelled. They chose their own mayor, formed alliances with the Saxons and the Frisians, and fought to remove themselves from the Austrasians. During the period of unrest Charles was able to escape from prison. Although Charles was only about twenty-five he had already become a popular figure among the Frankish people because of his demonstrated military prowess and bravery when assisting his father in battle. He assembled his forces, which included many who had been loyal to his father, and led them into battle against the Neustrians. He was at first unsuccessful, and the Neustrians were able to advance and force a surrender from Plectrude on behalf of her grandson. However, Charles secured his position as mayor of the palace in Austrasia.

Once he had gained control in Austrasia he vigorously began to extend his dominion. He defeated the Neustrians, forced the inhabitants of Burgundy to submit to his authority, and formed an alliance with Duke Odo of Aquitaine. By 720 he had reunited the three Frankish kingdoms, and his power and authority continued to increase. To preserve and expand his realm he was continually involved in war, most often against the Saxons and Frisians. With each successful battle Charles' reputation as a great military leader grew. His warriors became more and more highly skilled, disciplined, and devoted to him. All of this time, while still officially being the mayor of the palace, he was performing the duties of a king. In addition to commanding the army, he administered justice, issued decrees, oversaw civil and ecclesiastical appointments, and decided critical issues. Though he did rule for a short time without a king, the Merovingians continued to assume the official kingship throughout his years of governing.

This map of the Frankish domains at the time of Charles Martel is from *A Short History of the World* by H.G. Wells. (Wikimedia Commons)

The battle for which Charles Martel and his military forces are most celebrated took place in 732. It became known as the Battle of Tours or the Battle of Poitiers. About twenty years earlier the Arabs, or Saracens, had conquered Spain. In the years that followed they had crossed the Pyrenees and attempted to advance into Gaul. Duke Odo of Aquitaine had managed to stop their invasions for many years, but in 732 a new Arab leader started the attacks anew. The Arabs invaded and defeated Odo at Bordeaux. The city was plundered, the Christians slaughtered, and the whole area devastated. Odo sought help from the Franks.

Charles gathered his army and marched towards Aquitaine. The two forces, Franks and Arabs, met between the cities of Poitiers and Tours. For six days very little happened, as both sides evaluated the situation. On the seventh day there was a mighty battle. Charles chose to form his men in a defensive phalanx-like formation as they began. They were facing an armored force on horseback that greatly outnumbered them, but his disciplined Frankish infantry warriors were able to withstand the repeated charges of the enemy cavalry. Also, Charles had sent scouts to the Saracen base camp to free as many prisoners as possible. The Arabs became aware that their spoils from previous ravaging in the south was at risk, and some of them began to return to camp. Others thought there was a retreat and joined in. As the Saracen commander attempted to control his forces and stop the retreat he became surrounded by the Franks and was killed. The remaining Saracens then retreated. When the enemy did not return to fight the following morning, it became clear that Charles had won a very decisive victory. It was as a result of that battle, in which Charles' army broke and crushed the power of the enemy, that Charles earned the name Martel, which is the French word for hammer.

This painting by Carl von Steuben shows Charles Martel fighting in the Battle of Tours. (Wikimedia Commons)

Many years later it was recognized that Charles Martel, by stopping the advance of the Saracens, had preserved Christianity as the religion of Europe. Ironically, the church did not join in hailing Charles Martel as a hero. Early in his reign Charles had become aware that he would need to have a permanent, well-trained army in order to defend his kingdom and dominate their region. The bishops and abbots who had previously benefitted from his gifts and donations of land resented when some of those revenues were later diverted to support and reward the military. Annoyance because of the manner in which their assets were taken overrode appreciation of the fact that he was responsible for saving Europe from the Arab conquests.

In the years that followed the battle of Tours Charles continued to engage in campaigns in the south to drive the Saracens over the Pyrenees and to insure that they were unable to advance back into the Frankish territory. He also continued his battles in the north to subdue the pagan Germanic tribes. In 741 he divided his kingdom between his two sons, Carloman and Pippin. Shortly after that, on October 22nd, he died at his villa in Quierzy on the Oise River. He was buried at the Abbey of St. Denis.

Although Charles Martel is most famous for his victory at the Battle of Tours because of the important impact it had on history, his influence goes well beyond that one battle. In the area of religion, in addition to preserving Christianity as the religion of Europe by halting the Arab onslaught, he spread Christianity in Europe through his protection of Boniface. He supported Boniface's missionary work as he strove to eliminate paganism within the Germanic tribes. The close relationship between the popes and the Frankish rulers began during Charles' leadership. Pope Gregory III asked Charles for help as he tried to defend himself against the Lombards and offered to give him the Roman consulate. Although Charles refused, the new papal policy was set. This would later lead to his grandson, Charlemagne, being proclaimed Holy Roman Emperor.

Charles is credited with being the founder of feudalism. He caused a redistribution of land and change to internal administration when he established a standing army whose families needed to be supported. Lands, which were reclaimed from the church, were given to his military followers. Those parcels of land were the precursors to the fiefs which developed later in the Middle Ages. As Charles incorporated armored cavalry into his army, classes of fighters developed. Rules of vassalage began to be more clearly defined during Charles' years.

The authority of the position of mayor of the palace increased during Charles' time in that office. During Charles' final few years he chose to rule without a king, but did not himself become king. Charles Martel was the founder of the Carolingian line of kings who succeeded the Merovingians as rulers of the Franks. Charles' son Pippin deposed the Merovingian king, and the Carolinginian dynasty began its reign.

Charles Martel was the epitome of a great military leader. He was considered a brilliant general, and is famous for many of the military tactics he employed. He used the strategy of feigned retreat; he recognized the importance of the element of surprise, and was known for his ability to attack where and when he was least expected and to move far faster than his opponents would predict; he anticipated the dangers of his foes and prepared his men well; he was able to adapt and modify his plans as conditions of battle changed; he developed a standing permanent army of well-trained, disciplined, and loyal men; he incorporated heavy armed cavalry into his army, creating the first western knights. All of those things combined to enable him to be undefeated from 716 until his death in 741, even though he was always outnumbered. He unified the Franks and brought stability to a very volatile area. Charles Martel was one of history's most illustrious leaders.

The Palace of Versailles contains this statue of Charles Martel. (Wikimedia Commons)

9

Joseph of Arimathea

Joseph of Arimathea, a great-uncle of Jesus, was the 48th great-grandfather of Alice de Plumpton.

Joseph of Arimathea

Anna

Penarddun

Bran

Caractacus

Cyllin

Ystradwl

Althildis

Clodimir IV

Farabert

Sunno

Hilderic

Bartherus

Clodius III

Walter

Dagobert I

Genebald

Dagobert II

Clodius

Marcomir

Pharmond

Clodius

Sigimerus

Ferreolus

Ausbert

Arnoldus

St. Arnulf

Anchises

Pippin

Charles Martel

Pippin

Charlemagne

Pippin

Bernard

Pippin

Herbert I

Herbert II

Albert I

Herbert III

Otho

Herbert IV

Adelaide de Vermandois

Isabel de Vermandois

Ada de Warenne

William I, The Lion, King of Scotland

Isabella of Scotland

William de Ros

William de Ros

Lucy de Ros

William de Plumpton

Alice de Plumpton

Joseph of Arimathea is most commonly known because of the biblical references to his role in the burial of Yeshua. (Throughout this chapter we will refer to Yeshua as Jesus, which is the Hellenized form of the Aramaic name and the form that is most recognized today.) However, very few details about Joseph himself are included in the Bible, so it has been necessary to conduct extensive research to find out more about this extraordinary man and his life. From the factual information that has been discovered a biographical sketch emerges.

Joseph was the son of Matthat and his second wife, Rachel of Arimathea. He was a direct descendant of King David of Israel, and he was referred to as a Prince of David.

Joseph of Arimathea was also directly descended from Aaron, the older brother of Moses. Aaron had an important priestly role after Moses received instructions from God. One of his duties was to maintain the lampstand, or Menorah, in the Tabernacle.

> The Menorah was intended for use in the Tabernacle and then later in Solomon's Temple. The instructions concerning the Menorah that Moses received from God on Mt. Sinai were: "thou shalt make a candlestick of pure gold: his shaft and his branches, his bowls, his knops and his flowers shall be of the same. And six branches shall come out of the sides of it; three branches...out of the one side, and three branches...out of the other side." (Exodus 25: 31-32) The Menorah represented the ideal of universal enlightenment with the central lamp representing the light of God. The other six lamps represented the branches of human knowledge. Aaron had the duty of maintaining the Menorah lamps. "Aaron and his sons shall order it from evening to morning before the Lord: it shall be a statute for...the children of Israel." (Exodus 27: 21)

This is the presumed appearance of the first Menorah in the Tabernacle. (Wikimedia Commons)

Aaron was the first high priest of the Israelites and a great-grandson of Levi (one of the twelve sons of Jacob) who was the founder of one of the Twelve Tribes of Israel, the tribe of Levi. Aaron was the direct ancestor of all of the Israelite priests. Joseph of Arimathea's descent from Aaron was through Zadok, the high priest of King David of Israel. His descent from Aaron was also through the daughter of Simon "The Just," who married into Joseph of Arimathea's ancestral line from David.

(Wikimedia Commons)

Aaron

Eleazer

Phineas

Abishuah

Bukki

Uzzi

Zerahiah

Merioth

Amariah

Ahitub

Zadok

Ahimaaz

Azariah

Johanon

Azariah

Amariah

Ahitub

Merioth

Zadok

Azariah

Hilkiah

Azariah

Seriah

Josedech

Joshuah

Joachim

Eliashib

Jeiadah

Johanon

Juddual

Onias

Simon "The Just"

Daughter of Simon "The Just"

Janna

Melchi

Levi

Matthat

Joseph of Arimathea

Joseph of Arimathea was, therefore, a direct descendant of both the greatest king and the first high priest of Israel, as well as a direct descendant of both Judah and Levi, the founders of two of the Twelve Tribes of Israel.

Joseph was born in the town of Arimathea, now known as Ramallah, which was about six miles north of Jerusalem.

The town of Arimathea is shown just north of Jerusalem in this section of Rigobert Bonne's "Map of the New Testament Lands," published in 1771, which focuses on Judea at the time of King Herod.   (Wikimedia Commons)

Joseph of Arimathea was married to Alyuba, and they had two children, a daughter Anna and a son Josephes. His much older half-brother, Heli (the name is linguistically the same as Joachim), was the father of Mary and the grandfather of Jesus. Joseph of Arimathea became the guardian of Jesus after Joseph "the carpenter" died when Jesus was about twelve years old.

This is a section of an 1884 painting by Heinrich Hofmann showing Jesus at age twelve. (Wikimedia Commons)

Joseph of Arimathea was a prominent and extremely wealthy member of society. The high regard with which he was held is revealed by the title, "Marmore," that was used to refer to him and means great lord. He was the Roman Minister of Mines who was in charge of the mining and trading of metals, and he owned the ships used to transport those raw materials. Tin and lead were the valued metals of those times, and Joseph was in a position to influence the movement of those metals throughout the Mediterranean area, and from mines in Cornwall and Somerset in Britain to other areas in the Roman Empire. Joseph himself traveled widely and had influential contacts far beyond his place of birth, especially in Britain where he was known and highly respected by King Arviragus, a Druid King of Siluria, and his royal family. The Silurians were descendants of one of the Lost Tribes of Israel.

Joseph of Arimathea was also a member of the Sanhedrin, the Jewish (see detailed information about this word on the next page) ruling council.

The complex and often misunderstood words "Jew," "Jews," and "Jewish," are used today to designate individuals following the religion of "Judaism," or from that heritage. However, these words, as well as the words "Semite," "Hebrew," "Israelite," and "Judahite," have specific connotations. Abraham, along with his son Isaac and his grandson Jacob, were <u>Hebrews</u>, a word which came from an ancestor of Abraham named Eber. Before Eber the ancestors of Abraham were <u>Semites</u>, being descended from Shem, a son of Noah. <u>Israelites</u> are from Jacob (later given the name Israel by God) (Genesis 32:28) beginning with his sons who were the founders of the Tribes of Israel, and their descendants. For example, Moses and Aaron were Israelites since they were descended from Levi, the founder of the Tribe of Levi and a son of Jacob. God made a covenant with the Israelites, and they were the ones who were called the chosen people of God. <u>Judahites</u> are Israelites but specifically the descendants of Judah, the founder of the Tribe of Judah, one of the Tribes of Israel. <u>Judaism</u> became the term for the religion of the Jews which evolved from the religion of the Old Testament. The religion of the Old Testament was based on the Law of Moses and was the religion of Jesus which he worked to correct and return to its original meaning. Judaism is now a religion based on the Talmud and the beliefs and philosophy of the Pharisees who were predominately Edomites and not Israelites. The word "Jew" was not used in the entire original text of the Bible, only in the modern translations and in those the word "Jews" was first used in the book of 2 Kings 16:6. The word "Jew" in the Bible referred to a person from Judea, a region which included people with many different ethnicities. The term was not significant in biblical history until after the remnants of the original descendants of the Tribes of Judah and Benjamin returned following the Babylonian Captivity about 536 B.C. Mixed in with those returning people were many thousands of mixed multitude, or non-Israelite people, who became known as Jews. Also, the lands of the Tribes of Judah and Benjamin had been taken over by Edomites during the Captivity period. Those Edomites were not born of Israelites but rather were descended from Esau, the brother of Jacob. But they were also referred to as Jews after they were mixed in with the others after the return of the exiles from Babylon. Many of those later fled to North Africa and then to Spain. Those "Jews" became known as Sephardic Jews and later lived primarily in western Europe. Some scholars believe that over 80% of living Jews in the world today are descended from the Turkish-Mongolian tribes of the 8th century called Khazars who lived in southern Russia. Many of those pagan Khazars adopted Judaism as their religion. They were then considered to be Jews. The Khazars then spread through eastern Europe over the following centuries. Their descendants are called Ashkenazi Jews. But recent DNA analyses undermine the Khazars claim. Several Y-DNA studies have been conducted, and it has been determined that about 75% of all Jewish men have Middle Eastern ancestry. Jews, except for converts from other ethnicities, do have a common ancestry, and are a distinct population, originating in the Middle East. Very few, however, descend from Judah or any of the Tribes of Israel. **Joseph of Arimathea, Jesus, and Mary (the mother of Jesus) were not Jews but were actually Judahites, as well as Israelites, as they were descended from Judah through David. They were also Israelites because they were descended from Levi through Aaron and Zadok.** In this chapter we have used the terms Judahites, Israelites, and the religion of the Old Testament in order to be historically correct. The words "Jew," "Jews," and "Jewish" are used in those instances where the meaning in the time period involved would appear to be accurate.

Joseph of Arimathea was a very pious individual, and was one of the Essene brethren. Jesus and his immediate family also shared many of the Essene beliefs, and may have actually been of the Essene brethren also.

During this time in history Judaism was composed of four major sects, in addition to many smaller sub-sects. Certain general beliefs were common to all of these Jewish groups. They believed in the omnipotence of one God, the creator of everything. They believed that certain individuals were prophets, who were given insight from God and were able to prophesy future events. They believed that the greatest of these prophets was Moses, and that God had imparted unto Moses the laws which all Jews must follow. They believed that those instructions which were inscribed in the Torah were the Word of God. The Jewish people believed that a king of Israel, The Messiah, would emerge from the line of David through Solomon, as prophesied. They believed that The Messiah would be a powerful military leader who would save them from their current Roman oppression and bring peace. They did not believe that their Messiah would be divine. Most of the

Jewish people believed in resurrection, not only in terms of an individual's life after death, but as the ultimate triumph of good over evil.

The four main sects of Judaism during the time of Joseph of Arimathea were the Pharisees, the Sadducees, the Zealots, and the Essenes. These groups all shared the basic beliefs of the religion of the Old Testament, but had areas of disagreement over specific beliefs and practices.

The Pharisees made up the largest group. There were many diverse types of Pharisees, but they generally believed in the strict adherence to the laws of the Torah and that holiness was available to everyone, not just the priests. The Pharisees stressed the teaching of the religious laws to all young Jewish men. The Pharisees were predominately Edomites and were not descended from Israelites but from Esau, the brother of Jacob.

The Sadducees were the aristocratic priests. They placed great importance on the ceremonial aspects of religion and interpreted the Torah literally. They differed from the other sects in that they did not believe in life after death.

The Zealots were a militant sect that sought to free the Jews from Roman oppression, and to bring about equality among all of the people.

The Essenes were a learned group who believed in leading a very strict religious life. They believed in the immortality of the soul in an afterlife of reward or punishment, but they did not believe in a bodily resurrection. Some of the members of this sect withdrew from regular society and lived a communal existence. The Essenes were waiting for the Kingdom of God.

The successful and well-regarded Joseph of Arimathea, the great-uncle and guardian of Jesus, would have known his great-nephew well. His convictions regarding Jesus would have been based on his own religious heritage and study, as well as his personal knowledge of Jesus.

<u>Joseph of Arimathea would have considered that the actual and genetic parents of Jesus were Mary and Joseph "the carpenter."</u>

Many of the beliefs that are now included in Christian doctrine were not beliefs held by the contemporaries of Jesus, but were added long after his crucifixion. The earliest biblical inclusion of the virgin birth of Jesus was in the Gospel of Matthew which was written about 85 A.D. Matthew's earlier Gospel of the Hebrews did not include any mention of the virgin birth of Jesus. In Matthew 1:23 it is stated: "Behold, a virgin shall be with child, and shall bring forth a son, and they shall call his name Emmanuel, which being interpreted is, God with us." Matthew was trying to use the prophecy of Isaiah 7:14 to show that Isaiah was speaking about the birth of Jesus, but actually he was speaking about a child to be born in the 8th century B.C. Isaiah used the Hebrew word "almah" which means "young woman" but when Matthew utilized this prophecy and translated it into Greek he incorrectly translated the Hebrew word "almah" as "virgin" instead of the correct words "young woman." That is how the virgin birth story was first included, and it was then used to enhance the proposition that Jesus was divine. It also was used to work around the awkward situation involving the descent of Joseph "the carpenter" from David but through Jeconiah, which would preclude any descendant of his to sit on the Throne of David, in line with the prophecy of Jeremiah. (Jeremiah 22:30) The individuals involved in the Nazarene Ecclesia in Jerusalem led by James did not believe that Jesus was born of a virgin. James, himself, did not believe that; and he would have known, being the brother of Jesus. It appears the author or authors of the Gospel of John, written several years after Matthew and Luke, rejected the virgin birth of Jesus as either a mistake in those two gospels or as a made up myth. Jesus is clearly described as "the son of Joseph" in John 1:45.

In keeping with his religious beliefs, Joseph of Arimathea would have viewed Jesus as an extraordinary and inspired man but definitely not a divine being.

One of the basic tenets of the religion of the Old Testament was the oneness of God. To believe that a human was also divine would have been considered idolatrous. A man could not be God, and likewise God could not be a man. "God is not a man..." (Numbers 23:19) Jesus himself stated: "The first of all the commandments is, 'Hear, O Israel: The Lord our God is one Lord....'" (Mark 12:29 based on Deuteronomy 6:4) The deification of Jesus became a part of Christian doctrine many years later. Although some references in the New Testament imply the concept of divinity, most scholars consider those to be misinterpretations attributable to faulty translations. The

> Apostles Creed, which is believed to have originated during the late second century, does not include any mention of the divinity of Jesus. It was not until the Council of Nicaea in 325 A.D. that the divine nature of Jesus became an official part of Christian doctrine.

Many of Jesus' followers considered him to be The Messiah, but Joseph of Arimathea would not have believed this.

> Joseph of Arimathea would have been intimately aware of his shared genealogy with Jesus, and he would have realized that the ancestry of Jesus did not satisfy all of the hereditary criteria which the prophecies deemed necessary for an individual to qualify to be The Messiah. It is true that Jesus was descended from David in his father's (Joseph "the carpenter") direct male line. And it is true that the descent from David was through Solomon in line with prophecy (I Chronicles 28:5-7). But it is also true that Jeconiah (Matthew 1:11) was in his male line going back to David. So Jesus descended from David through Jeconiah, and prophecy mandated that no descendant of Jeconiah could ever sit on the throne of David and rule as The Messiah. (Jeremiah 22:30).

At the time of Jesus the concept of the Trinity had not yet been created. It is certain that Joseph of Arimathea would not have believed in it.

> The concept of the Trinity developed over a period of time to become a doctrine whose belief is now foundational for a Christian. The Trinity had not evolved up to the fourth century, but under the rule of the Roman emperor Constantine, many beliefs were grafted on to the already compromised religion which had by then completely adapted to the Gentile environment and had become corrupted by paganism. The Council of Constantinople in 360 A.D. created the Trinity in its approved form. The term Trinity does not appear in the New Testament, and the followers of Jesus would never have heard of it. Joseph of Arimathea and his fellow believers of the first century, including Jesus, would have considered the doctrine of the Trinity to be blasphemous and against their monotheistic beliefs.

Joseph of Arimathea, himself a learned religious scholar, was involved with Jesus as his great-uncle and guardian, but he was not an active supporter and follower of Jesus during his ministry. His heritage and personal religious studies would have resulted in his having strict and conservative interpretations of the Law of Moses. Also, Joseph had positions of respect within both his religious culture and the Roman business and political structure. His high status within those communities would have been dependent upon his ability to demonstrate beliefs and behaviors acceptable to those groups. However, at the time of the crucifixion, Joseph's family loyalty dictated that he play a major role. That dedication to his family changed his life dramatically.

Heinrich Hofmann depicted Joseph of Arimathea prior to the burial of Jesus. (Wikimedia Commons)

Joseph of Arimathea is mentioned in each of the four Gospels of the Bible. Those are the only biblical references to him, and each is a description of his involvement in the burial of Jesus. The following citations are from the King James Version:

> "When the even was come there came a rich man of Arimathea, named Joseph, who also himself was Jesus' disciple: He went to Pilate, and begged the body of Jesus. Then Pilate commanded the body to be delivered. And when Joseph had taken the body, he wrapped it in a clean linen cloth, And laid it in his own new tomb, which he had hewn out in the rock: and he rolled a great stone to the door of the sepulchre, and departed." (Matthew 27:57 -60)
>
> "Joseph of Arimathea, an honorable counseller, which also waited for the kingdom of God, came, and went in boldly unto Pilate, and craved the body of Jesus. And Pilate marvelled if he were already dead: and calling unto him the centurion, he asked him whether he had been any while dead. And when he knew it of the centurion, he gave the body to Joseph. And he brought fine linen, and took him down, and wrapped him in the linen, and laid him in a sepulchre which was hewn out of a rock, and rolled a stone unto the door of the sepulchre." (Mark 15:43-46)
>
> "And, behold, there was a man named Joseph, a counseller; and he was a good man, and a just: (The same had not consented to the counsel and deed of them;) he was of Arimathea, a city of the Jews: who also himself waited for the kingdom of God. This man went unto Pilate, and begged the body of Jesus. And he took it down, and wrapped it in linen, and laid it in a sepulchre that was hewn in stone, wherein never man before was laid." (Luke 23:50-53)
>
> "And after this Joseph of Arimathea, being a disciple of Jesus, but secretly for fear of the Jews, besought Pilate that he might take away the body of Jesus: and Pilate gave him leave. He came therefore, and took the body of Jesus." (John 19:38)

During the period of time following the crucifixion the followers of Jesus were in grave danger, and many had to flee to seek safety. Joseph of Arimathea used his influence, wealth, and contacts to provide protection for some of the closest supporters and family members of Jesus. Together they traveled to Caesarea (as seen on the map on page 88 by R. Bonne), an active seaport on the Mediterranean coast, about seventy miles northwest of Jerusalem. It was a location of relative safety, dependent on the Roman officials ruling at the time.

Those who followed Jesus' teachings became known as the Followers of the Way, or the Nazarenes. (The word Nazarene comes from a Hebrew word which means descendant of Jesse, the father of King David of Israel.) One such Follower of the Way, or Nazarene, was Stephen, a believer who spoke boldly in support of the teachings of Jesus and who was accused of blasphemy and then tried by the Sanhedrin. He was stoned by an angry mob that was encouraged by Saul of Tarsus. Stephen is known as the first to be martyred for Jesus. News of the stoning of Stephen would have caused further desperation for Joseph of Arimathea and his companions.

Joseph, although having some degree of security stemming from his position as a Roman minister, had himself become a target of the Sanhedrin because of his overt actions on behalf of Jesus and his family after the crucifixion. Ultimately Joseph of Arimathea and his companions were apprehended in Caesarea and forced out to sea in a boat having neither sails nor oars. There were about fourteen passengers who accompanied Joseph. Those included Lazarus and his sisters, Mary Magdalene and Martha, as well as Mary, the mother of Jesus, who had been protected by Joseph for some time.

As mentioned previously, the Gospels provide information about Joseph's involvement with Jesus at the time of the crucifixion, but do not relate details of Joseph's life before or after that. One of the most respected sources of information pertaining to Joseph of Arimathea's departure from Caesarea is *Annales Ecclesiastici*, a history written by Caesar Baronius during the years 1588 to 1607. Cardinal Baronius was an Italian historian and Librarian of the Vatican near the end of the sixteenth century. He was asked by Roman Catholic Church leaders to write a history to counter the prominent church history of that era which had been written by Lutheran scholars. Ironically, Baronius is renowned for his honest efforts to provide truthful and unbiased information in his monumental history. Baronius, in referring to his history, said: "I have been most careful to guard against obscuring the pure truth by putting in anything doubtful." Baronius' history included an account of Joseph's forced trip by boat in volume one, section five, page 208, under the heading for the year A.D. 35.

The Jewish officials who put Joseph and his companions out to sea lacked the authority to sentence them to death and felt that was a means of placing their fate in God's hands, a fate which would seem to be death. However, the boat reached land, most likely because of assistance rendered by seamen who knew Joseph and followed covertly in other vessels. Joseph's boat landed in Cyrene, a Mediterranean seaport located in what is now Libya. The travelers refitted their ship and continued on across the Mediterranean Sea, landing at Crete, Sicily, near Rome, and then Marseilles.

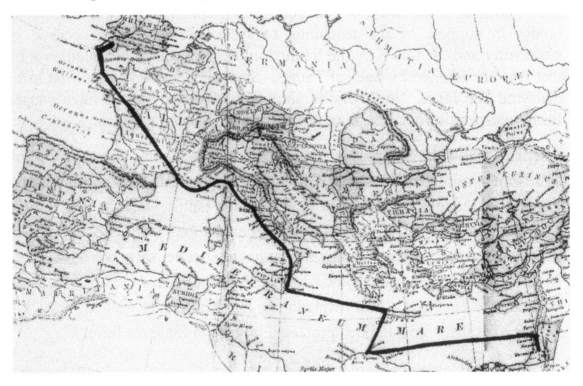

This section of a map of the Roman Empire by George R. Crooks in 1897 was modified by the authors to show the journey of Joseph of Arimathea and his companions in the year 35 A.D. from Jerusalem to the Isle of Avalon. (Wikimedia Commons)

From Marseilles Joseph of Arimathea and most of his companions set out towards Britain. Britain was considered by Joseph to be the safest place in the known world to avoid persecution by either the Romans or the Jews. They traveled up the Rhone and then by land across Gaul on a route familiar to Joseph from his previous tin trading trips. This thirty-day journey through Gaul included a stop at Limoges. They arrived in Brittany at Morlaix, then boarded sailing vessels and crossed the body of water now known as the English Channel to Cornwall. From there they traveled overland approaching the Isle of Avalon, which is now known as Glastonbury, England. Then they boarded small boats to reach the island. This part of the journey would have been especially treacherous since it was not a part of the familiar trading route. After traveling more than twenty-five hundred miles from Caesarea they were welcomed at the Isle of Avalon by King Arviragus, who presented each individual arriving with a large plot of land. This land would remain tax free in perpetuity, as is verified in the

Domesday Book which was compiled for William the Conqueror and completed in the year 1086.

Joseph had been asked by the apostle Philip to establish a place of worship in Britain where descendants of the Lost Tribes of Israel could be introduced to the teachings of Jesus. This was consistent with the request of Jesus that his followers spread his message among the Lost Tribes.

> "These twelve Jesus sent forth, and commanded them, saying, Go not into the way of the Gentiles, and into any city of the Samaritans enter ye not: But go rather to the lost sheep of the house of Israel." (Matthew 10:5-6) It is clear that Jesus was telling his disciples to limit their contact to the Israelites who were the twelve tribes that came down from Jacob's sons. While this position is disputed by some Christians who believe that the emphasis was on the Gentiles, it is certainly verified by the salutation of the General Epistle of James. This was possibly among the earliest of the New Testament writings, dating from about 50 A.D., and was written by James, the brother of Jesus. He, of course, would have known the intention of Jesus and in the salutation of his epistle he stated: "to the twelve tribes which are scattered abroad, greeting." (James 1:1) So Jesus wanted his message to go to the Israelites only, the descendants of the Twelve Tribes of Israel. This excluded the Jews, meaning those mixed ancestry people living in Judea, and the Gentiles who were not descended from the twelve tribes.

Eventually Joseph of Arimathea established a Nazarene synagogue to carry out this mission. A primitive building was constructed in which they could praise God and practice their beliefs. Of course, the teachings of Jesus were an integral part of the worship services, especially those ideas included in the Sermon on the Mount. The teachings of this Nazarene synagogue were epitomized by this triad which was written by Lazarus and quoted at that time:

> "Believe in God who made thee;
> Love God who saved thee;
> Fear God who will judge thee."

Joseph of Arimathea was an inspiring figure, and he had a powerful message about seeking the Kingdom of God. The Druids welcomed his information and insights. Joseph was able to give a first-hand account of the teachings of Jesus.

While Joseph was establishing a worship place in Britain, James, the brother of Jesus, had become the leader of the Nazarenes back in Jerusalem.

There would, undoubtedly, have been communication (though limited and difficult) between James and Joseph of Arimathea, especially since James' mother was one of those who had accompanied Joseph and was living on the Isle of Avalon.

James, the Just, was the brother of Jesus.   (Wikimedia Commons)

This image of Mary, the mother of Jesus, is part of a painting by Leonardo da Vinci.   (Wikimedia Commons)

Mary, the mother of Jesus and James and their other brothers and sisters, was known while a young Judahite girl by her Hebrew name, Miryam. However, she is most often known and recognized today by the name Mary. Mary was the daughter of Heli and his wife, Anna. Mary traveled with her uncle, Joseph of Arimathea, to the Isle of Avalon in Britain in 35 A.D. She lived out her life in that protected and relatively safe environment, died a natural death in 48 A.D., and was buried in the primitive synagogue on the Isle of Avalon. Most people view the later life of Mary as a great mystery. Over the years there have been empty tombs discovered in various places which were said to be Mary's and were purported to prove that Mary was assumed, both body and soul, into heaven. That was a tradition for many years, but there is no actual reference to the assumption of Mary in the Bible, and the idea was condemned as heretical by two popes in the fifth and sixth centuries. However, the tradition continued, and since the seventh century the belief in the bodily assumption of Mary was allowed, even though the Vatican has been aware since that time of the likelihood that Mary was actually buried in Britain on the Isle of Avalon. In November of 1950, Pope Pius XII declared that the Assumption of Mary is a dogma of the Roman Catholic Church and threatened that, since it was then a required belief, any dissenter is an apostate who has fallen away completely from the Church. That formalization of what had previously been only a tradition discouraged investigations that would weaken the Church's position. Admitting Mary's existence in Britain and her participation in spreading her knowledge of the beliefs of Jesus would contradict what had become a fundamental belief of Roman Catholicism. But Mary did live and die as any other human being would. In the Bible Mary was mentioned only one time after the crucifixion of Jesus. That was when she joined the disciples in the upper room for prayer, as related in Acts 1:14. After that she disappeared from the Gospels. The reason for that is not that she had been assumed into heaven, but that she had moved away with other family members and supporters of Jesus, staying at Caesarea for a while and then enduring the lengthy trip all the way to the Isle of Avalon in Britain, where she remained until her death about thirteen years later.

Joseph was very successful in providing protection for those who had fled to the Isle of Avalon with him, and he was successful in converting many of the Britons to his Old Testament beliefs which now included the teachings of Jesus. Joseph's ministry in Britain would have been very similar to the work of James back in Jerusalem.

However, the basic beliefs that both men espoused were being challenged by another person, one who falsely claimed to be an apostle of Jesus. (Revelation 21:14) That person was Paul of Tarsus. Paul, previously known as Saul, had been among those who persecuted the followers of Jesus. About the year A.D. 36 Paul proclaimed himself to have become a supporter of Jesus. James and the other followers of Jesus were wary of Paul, who had been their enemy, and as Paul became more deeply involved with them it became apparent that his mission was different than theirs. Eventually a rift developed among the supporters of Jesus. Some continued to follow the Law of Moses while embracing the teachings of Jesus, as James and Joseph of Arimathea did. Others began to follow Paul and accept his teachings as they were presented to the Gentiles. Those teachings included an emphasis on the sacrificial nature of the death of Jesus and the supremacy of faith over good works, unlike James' (the brother of Jesus) belief in good works and not just in faith. This was because Paul could relate to the evil of mankind since he was an admittedly evil individual himself.

> "For the good that I would I do not: but the evil which I would not, that I do." (Romans 7: 19)

Jesus had warned his disciples to beware of false prophets who would replace his teachings with their own.

> "Beware of false prophets, which come to you in sheep's clothing, but inwardly they are ravening wolves." (Matthew 7:15)

Paul was the type of false prophet that Jesus warned would be changing his beliefs and teachings and forming a belief system that he (Jesus) would not have approved of. (Some believe that Matthew 7:15 was a specific reference to Paul, whom Jesus never knew. Paul claimed to be a Benjaminite, and the symbol for the Tribe of Benjamin was a wolf.) The message of Jesus was for everyone to keep the commandments of God. (Matthew 5:19) Paul encouraged the Gentiles not to follow God's laws. (Acts 21:28) This is the greatest example of the false teachings of Paul and his followers, and Jesus would have condemned it.

Paul of Tarsus was the individual who was actually responsible for the founding and growth of what became known as Christianity. Modern Christianity is based largely on Paul's vision and interpretations. What began as an effort by Jesus to purify and restore the religion of the Old Testament became a religion for Gentiles because of Paul's powerful influence. (Contrary to what present day Christians think and contrary to what Paul himself claimed, some members of early Jewish sects that followed the teachings of Jesus believed that Paul was born a Gentile. They believed he converted to Judaism in order to marry a daughter of a high priest. The process of conversion required that he be circumcised. Even after he had submitted to that requirement, however, the young lady refused to marry Paul. He became enraged and thereafter argued against circumcision and against the Mosaic Law, both orally and in his writings. Paul was unaware of some basic ideas and practices included in the Old Testament, and he was most comfortable with pagan beliefs.) Paul, while named Saul, had been a persecutor of the Nazarenes, those who had followed Jesus and those who joined the group after the crucifixion. He inflamed the crowd, urging the stoning of Stephen in A.D. 35. He had a violent confrontation with James the brother of Jesus, throwing him down the steps of the Temple, a confrontation which James never got over for the rest of his life. Paul claimed to have known Jesus from a vision and used that association in about A.D. 39 to infiltrate the Followers of the Way, the group who had walked with Jesus, including Jesus' actual family members. This attempt to usurp the belief system away from the followers of Jesus and the family of Jesus resulted in a major power struggle in the period from about A.D. 39 to A.D. 49. According to references in the Dead Sea Scrolls James "excommunicated" Paul from the Ecclesia. A.D. 49 became the turning point when the Pauline-Gentile movement would start growing because of Paul's influence, and the Nazarene influence would become almost nonexistent. It was also at that time that the Gentiles, in what would later become the Pauline Christian Church, would start to turn on the Followers of the Way and even blame all Jews for the crucifixion of Jesus. The Followers of the Way, including Jesus' own family members, had no respect for those who were seizing control of the belief system of Jesus and their obvious hatred of the Jews. (By the time that the Gospels were written, twenty years or more after the death of Paul, his views had greatly influenced the Gospel writers, thereby posthumously changing the historical record to include his views in place of many of the actual truths.)

This painting by James Tissot portrays Joseph of Arimathea in his later years. (Wikimedia Commons)

Though Joseph of Arimathea was far removed geographically from James and his conflicts with Paul, it appears that he was still impacted by Paul's increasing influence. Joseph had been appointed by Philip, his dear friend, to be the Apostle to the Britons. However, Paul knew that Joseph of Arimathea's message about the teachings of Jesus conflicted with his own views, and he knew that this would frustrate his efforts to convert the people of Britain to the Pauline beliefs. So he found it necessary to send two of his devoted followers to carry his message to the Britons. Those two bishops sent by Paul were Simon Zelotes and Aristobulus. Those early two were followed by others in later years, and Paul's teachings ultimately prevailed over the Nazarene message that Joseph of Arimathea had spread, although not completely for several centuries.

Joseph of Arimathea lived peacefully in Britain for many years. In 82 A.D. Joseph died, and he was buried in the ancient synagogue on the Isle of Avalon. According to Maelgwyn, an uncle of Saint David, writing about 540 in his *Historia de Rebus Britannicis*, Joseph of Arimathea was buried over the burial plot of Mary, the mother of Jesus.

Joseph of Arimathea and his companions on the Isle of Avalon had avoided the very tragic and brutal treatment that befell the many disciples and relatives of Jesus who served throughout the Roman Empire. Almost all of the followers of Jesus who had scattered to spread his word met violent deaths. In fact, the Desposyni, the descendants of the close family members of Jesus, continued to be oppressed for many generations.

> The Desposyni were at first highly revered, despite the division that was developing among the supporters of Jesus in regard to following traditional religious laws as encouraged by the Nazarenes, or relaxing those beliefs in order to appeal to the Gentiles as Paul insisted. After James, the brother of Jesus, was killed in 62 A.D., Simeon succeeded him as the head of the Nazarenes in Jerusalem. (The Rev. Robert Taylor in his book, *The Diegesis; Being a Discovery of the Origin, Evidences, and Early History of Christianity*, stated that "James...was killed by St. Paul [in 62 A.D., long after Paul's professed 'conversion']. Having been set by the Jews upon a pinnacle of the temple...Paul thrust him off.") Simeon was related to Jesus in two ways. First, he was his cousin, as he was the son of Cleophas, the younger brother of Joseph "the carpenter." Secondly, he was his half-brother, since Mary (the mother of Jesus) had married Cleophas after the death of Joseph "the carpenter" and was the mother of

Simeon. The Nazarenes continued to be led by succeeding generations of the family of Jesus. As time passed, however, the Roman Church felt increasingly threatened by the Desposyni. By the fourth century the teachings of Paul had evolved into the Roman Catholic Church which had become the official religion of the Roman Empire. Even while calling their religion Christianity, the Church, ironically, sought to eliminate the very people who were the most intimately related to Jesus, those who had descended from his close family members. Several centuries after the crucifixion the Desposyni had essentially disappeared, most of them having been hunted down and killed by agents of the Roman Catholic Church.

Joseph of Arimathea is known mostly for his biblical role in providing a tomb for Jesus, but he impacted history in other ways as well. He provided protection and safe passage for some of Jesus' closest followers and family members during the dangerous period following the crucifixion. He also spread the teachings of Jesus to the descendants of the Israelites living in Britain, some of whom carried that message throughout Gaul and even to Rome itself before Paul had first arrived there.

Before his death he would have become aware that the teachings of his great-nephew, Jesus, had been distorted by Paul and his followers, and that those distortions were developing into a religion (tainted by pagan practices and ideas from mystical religions such as Mithraism) that he and Jesus would not have accepted. They would not have accepted the religion that became known as Christianity. Joseph of Arimathea believed in Jesus because of his life. The later Christians believed in Jesus because of his death.

Joseph of Arimathea would have known that he, himself, had done his best to spread the true message of Jesus. Being descended from David of the royal line of Judah and from Aaron of the priestly line, both Jesus and Joseph of Arimathea were Israelites and of the religion of the Old Testament. It is amazing that today Jesus and Joseph of Arimathea are almost always thought to be connected only to Christianity. Very few people have any knowledge of the actual ancestry, heritage, religion and beliefs of Jesus and his great-uncle, Joseph of Arimathea.

10

King David of Israel

King David of Israel is one of the most illustrious and well-known figures in all of history, with abundant details of his life having been documented in the Bible. His name is mentioned more often than any other in the Bible. Stories about David are contained in various parts of the Old Testament, most notably in the two books of Samuel, the first book of Kings, and the first book of Chronicles. Seventy-three psalms are attributed to David, and there are numerous references to him in the New Testament. He is renowned as a ruler, a warrior, a poet, and a musician. King David of Israel was the originator of the prestigious Davidic Bloodline. He was the 87th great-grandfather of Alice de Plumpton.

David was born in Bethlehem about three thousand years ago. He was the youngest son of Jesse, whose lineage traced back to Abraham. Abraham, a Hebrew, is recognized as the first of his people to reject polytheism and accept the concept of one God. Abraham's son Isaac was the father of Jacob, whose name was changed to Israel. Jacob had twelve sons, Israelites, from whom the twelve separate tribes of Israel arose. One of those sons was Judah. Judah had twin sons, Pharez and Zerah, Judahites, and it was from Pharez that David was descended.

The lion was the symbol for the Israelite Tribe of Judah. (Wikimedia Commons)

Abraham and his family left Mesopotamia and inhabited Canaan, but widespread famine later forced his descendants to migrate into Egypt. At first they lived peacefully in Egypt, but eventually they were forced into slavery. The Old Testament book of Exodus tells of their escape. Moses led the Israelites out of Egypt and they wandered for forty years. During that time Moses received the Ten Commandments which delineated a code of conduct which should be followed, and they entered into a Covenant with God. Moses' older brother Aaron was his spokesman and became the first high priest of the Israelites. Both Moses and Aaron died during the years of wandering, and Joshua led the Israelites into their promised land where they defeated those already living there. The Israelite tribes at that time lived as independent groups without a centralized government, but a military and religious leader called a judge would lead the combined tribes in times of crisis. Samuel the prophet was such a religious leader. After many years, though, the continual threats from others in the area, especially from the Philistines, created a need for them to more formally organize themselves and join together under one strong military leader and ruler. Samuel ordained Saul, a member of the tribe of Benjamin, as the first king of the Israelites, in 1049 B.C. King Saul was successful in leading the Israelites to victory in battles against the Philistines and various other antagonists. However, Saul failed to obey God's instructions, as delivered to him by Samuel, and so the royal line of succession was not passed on to his son.

Samuel was told by God that the individual that would succeed Saul as king would be a son of Jesse who lived in Bethlehem. He arranged a meeting with Jesse and was introduced to seven of his eight sons, but realized that none of them was the chosen one. Samuel asked Jesse if he had any more sons, and Jesse told him that his youngest son was not there, but was tending the sheep. Then he summoned his youngest son, David, and presented him to Samuel. Recognizing that David was the future king that God intended, Samuel anointed him with oil, and so it was determined that the second king of Israel would be from the tribe of Judah.

David was a shepherd. While still a boy he was responsible for caring for his father's flock of sheep. The time he spent tending his sheep would have provided the opportunity for him to develop characteristics for which he later became famous. Courage and strength were needed to defend the sheep from predators. It is said that David fought off both a bear and a lion by himself in order to protect his flock. A shepherd spent long periods of time alone. This required self-reliance. This solitude also provided time that could be spent in meditation and in pursuing solitary interests and developing personal skills. Later in his life David was well-known for his poetry and his ability to play the harp.

As a young man David was called to the court of King Saul because of his reputation as a musician. Saul wanted a harpist who could play music to help relieve his tormented mind. David stayed near the king and played for him frequently. While dwelling in the palace he formed a close friendship with Jonathan, Saul's son. Saul himself grew more and more appreciative of David, because of the calming effect of his musical talent and also because of the bravery he demonstrated.

The Israelite army was involved in repeated battles with the Philistines. During one such conflict which took place in the Valley of Elah, the Philistines had a giant named Goliath who challenged the Israelites to send forward someone to fight him. His taunting continued for many days, but the Israelites could find no one with enough courage to vie one-on-one with an armored warrior so large. It happened that Jesse sent David to carry food to his older brothers who were serving in Saul's army, and David heard Goliath's challenge. He determined that he would be the one to represent the Israelites against the giant. He requested permission from King Saul, and convinced him that since he had previously slaughtered both a lion and a bear by himself he was capable of defeating Goliath. Saul attempted to dress David in his own armor, but it was too cumbersome for the youth. David chose to face Goliath with no armor and armed only with his staff, his slingshot, and some stones.

Goliath was astounded to see that such an unthreatening-looking opponent had taken up his challenge and he taunted him, but David responded that he would be victorious because God was with him. David slung his first stone, and it hit his foe in the forehead. Goliath tumbled to the ground, and David rushed forward and used the giant's own sword to behead him. When the Philistines saw that their champion had been defeated they fled, and the Israelites pursued them and triumphed over them.

This image of David, after having slayed Goliath, was included in Dore's English Bible. (Wikimedia Commons)

David's victory over Goliath brought him immediate fame. It also resulted in his being given a military command by King Saul. Eventually he rose in rank to become second in command, under Abner, the head of the army. David's continued successes further increased his popularity, both with the general population and within the royal palace. Jonathan and David's friendship grew even stronger, and Michal, the king's daughter, fell in love with him. The fame and admiration he received made Saul extremely jealous and fearful of David. His ill-feelings turned to hate, and he made repeated attempts to kill David both directly and through various plots in which he placed David in situations in which he thought his death would result. Michal, who had become David's wife, helped him escape one of her father's plans to kill him, and Jonathan warned him about another plot. Finally, the danger to David's life became so imminent that he was forced to flee rapidly, unarmed and without food.

David first sought help at Nob, the city of priests. There he did not reveal that he was being pursued by Saul. When Ahemelech the priest questioned why he was alone, David became frightened and made up a fictitious story to explain his solitary condition. He asked for bread and a weapon. The priest gave him bread from the consecrated table and Goliath's sword which was kept there. Then David continued his flight. When Saul later discovered that the priests had assisted David in his escape, though unknowingly, he ordered that all of the priests and others in the city of Nob be killed.

After David left Nob he entered the land of the Philistines, seeking refuge with Achise the king of Gath. The servants of the king recognized that he was David who had slain Goliath, and they warned Achise. When David realized that he was in danger, he feigned madness. His deception was successful, and he was able to leave unharmed.

David settled for a while in a cave of Adullum in the wilderness. He was joined there by his parents, other family members, and a growing band of followers. One of those who aligned himself with David was the priest Abiathar who was the sole survivor of the massacre at the sanctuary at Nob. As his forces grew in number and strength David began to exert his military might while, at the same time, eluding Saul.

Learning that the city of Keilah was about to be attacked by the Philistines, David and his men fought against the Philistines and saved the city. Saul heard about his presence in Keilah and assembled his armies to go to attack the city. David and his men, who numbered about six hundred at that time, left Keilah and fled once again from Saul and his army. They took refuge in the wilderness of Ziph to escape from him. Saul's son, Jonathan, sought David out in the woods, and consoled and encouraged him. The two friends made a covenant with each other, and then Jonathan returned to his home.

Despite the fact that King Saul was searching for David and trying to kill him, David continued to respect Saul as God's anointed. He strove to evade Saul and not to harm him. On two occasions David had the opportunity to kill Saul, and both times he refused. One time Saul discovered that David was in the wilderness of En-gedi. He took three thousand of his men and went in pursuit of David. When Saul entered a cave to rest, David and his companions were hiding nearby. This was an excellent opportunity for David to kill Saul; but, instead, he cautioned his men not to harm Saul and he himself went into the cave and secretly cut off the bottom edges of his garment as he slept. Then, when Saul awoke and began to walk away, David called after him. He revealed to Saul how he had spared his life and that he had no intention of ever harming him. Another time Saul pursued David in the wilderness of Ziph. When David learned that Saul and his troops had pitched their tents and were sleeping, he sneaked into their camp and located the spot where Saul was sleeping. David's companion wanted to kill Saul, but David stopped him. David then took Saul's sword and his jar of water without awakening anyone in the camp. When he was at a distance, he shouted to Abner the captain of Saul's army, and told him that he hadn't done a good job of protecting the king as he had been able to enter the camp and take Saul's sword. Saul heard David's voice and realized that once again David had spared him.

When David was in the wilderness of Paran, he sought support from a wealthy man named Nabel, who had thousands of sheep and goats. He sent a small group of his men to inquire whether he would share some of the food that he had for his shearers with David and his men. Nabel rudely rebuffed the men. When they reported back to David he was furious and decided to take revenge against Nabel. He and his men approached Nabel's property, intending to kill him and all those in his household. Nabel's wife, Abigail, heard about what had happened, and she secretly went out with her servants bearing bread and wine and other foods for David and his men. When she met David and his forces she spoke eloquently to David, reminding him of God's great plans for him and pointing out that he would regret the rash killings. David was very appreciative that she interceded to prevent his impetuous plans from being carried out. It happened that about ten days after this all transpired Nabel died. Then David sent for Abigail, and she became one of his wives.

David's existence as an exile in the wilderness continued for several years. Finally he again sought refuge with the Philistines. This time he was accepted by Achise of Gath, and David was given the town of Ziklag in which he and all of his men and their families could settle. This was a time of relative security for David. He was within the land of the Philistines and did not have to fear Saul, and he had the luxury of not having to continually move around through the wilderness. From their headquarters in Ziklag, David and his forces would ride out and attack various tribes that had been raiding towns in Judah. They would kill those enemies and return to Ziklag with the spoils of war – sheep, oxen, and camels. One of the tribes they attacked was the Amalekites.

Eventually Achise requested that David and his men join his army in a battle against King Saul's forces. This presented a difficult dilemma for David, but he started out with his men following Achise and his Philistine army. Before reaching their destination, however, Achise was convinced by his men that it was too big of a risk to rely on David's fidelity when fighting against Israel. David and his men were asked to turn back. When they arrived back in Ziklag they found that while they had been gone their town had been plundered and burned by the Amalekites and their families had been captured. David and his men were distraught and overcome with grief, but then David asked Abiathar the priest to bring the ephod and he inquired of God and decided to try to overtake the enemy and recover their families that had been taken. They found an Egyptian servant who had been abandoned by his Amalekite master because he had fallen ill. They fed him and enlisted his help. From the information he provided they were able to locate the Amalekites and kill them. They succeeded in rescuing all of their families and recovering everything that had been taken. Also, they collected the flocks and herds of the enemy and additional spoils. David shared the spoils of war with all those who had followed him to Ziklag, and he also sent gifts of the spoils to the elders in Judah.

Meanwhile, Achise and the Philistines had engaged the men of Israel in battle and had prevailed. Jonathan and two other sons of Saul were killed in the battle. Saul was seriously wounded by archers, and then fell on his own sword. It was a devastating defeat. Those of Israel who were not killed fled. The Philistines took over much of their land. When news of the battle reached Ziklag, David, and all of those with him, mourned the death of Saul and Jonathan and the others of the House of Israel.

David was no longer a fugitive with a small band of followers. During his years of flight from Saul he had amassed a strong fighting force and allied himself with some powerful families in Judah. After Saul's death he made his way back into Judah, succeeded in occupying it, and made Hebron in southern Judah his capital city. David ruled as king over the southern kingdom of Judah for over seven years. During this time Saul's son Ishbaal, with the support of Saul's military leader Abner, reigned over the northern tribes of Israel. The two kingdoms waged war against each other. As their battles continued, David's strength gradually increased as Ishbaal's power waned. Finally, after a quarrel between Abner and Ishbaal, Abner swung his support to David, and the war ended.

The pact between David and Abner was conditioned upon a promise from Ishbaal that his sister Michal would be returned to David. Michal, Saul's daughter, had married David before his escape to the wilderness. She did not accompany him when he fled, and her father gave her in marriage to another man, during David's long enforced absence. Michal was reunited with David, as Ishbaal had agreed. By the time that Michal returned to David he had six other wives and six sons.

David was king over all of Israel, as in *2* Samuel 5:1-12. (Wikimedia Commons)

Shortly after Abner decided to support David he was murdered by Joab, David's nephew. Joab killed Abner to avenge the death of his brother whom Abner had killed in battle. David was not a party to the killing of Abner, and greatly mourned his death. Soon after that Ishbaal was also murdered, but by two captains of his own forces. The assassins went to David expecting his approval since Ishbaal had been fighting against David for so many years, but David admonished them for killing God's anointed and ordered that they both be executed.

After the deaths of Abner and Ishbaal, elders from the tribes of Israel who had aligned themselves with Ishbaal came to David in Hebron and sought to become a part of his kingdom. In 1003 B.C. David became king of all Israel. He was thirty years old. One of the first things he did as king of the united kingdom of Judah and Israel was to move his capital city from Hebron. He moved northward and captured the city of Jerusalem from the Jebusites. Jerusalem, called Jebus at that time, was highly fortified. David and his men were able to breach the defenses of the city by entering through passageways that carried water from the Gihon Spring. Jerusalem became the City of David and the capital of Israel. Hiram, the king of Tyre, sent skilled workmen and building materials to erect a palace for David in his new capital city.

When the Philistines learned that David had become king of all Israel they waged war against his kingdom. David sought God's advice, as was his custom before taking up arms, and he felt confident that Israel would prevail. He had a well-organized army made up of very experienced, brave, and loyal warriors, commanded by Joab. His mighty fighting force was successful. The Philistines were vanquished and driven out of Israel. Although David had subdued the Philistines, conflicts with other neighboring nations continued for many years. David's forces were victorious, and his kingdom was greatly enlarged because of his victories. He also accumulated great wealth through the spoils of war and the tributes which were paid by the conquered nations.

King David recognized that Israel's security depended on God's blessing, and that obedience to God's laws was essential. Having established a secure place for his people, he knew that it was important then to have the Ark of the Covenant brought into Jerusalem. David gathered his people from all over Israel to accompany him, and they went together and got the Ark of the Covenant from its previous location in Baalah of Judah. It was a very festive occasion with the people singing and dancing and playing musical instruments as they moved along. The Ark was carried on a cart that was pulled by oxen, and at one point the oxen stumbled. Uzza, who was one of those driving the cart, reached out to keep the Ark from falling. When he touched the Ark he immediately fell over dead. David was very upset, for he realized then that they had displeased God by not following the proper procedure for moving the Ark. David decided to not bring the Ark the rest of the way to Jerusalem yet. Instead, he left it at the house of Obed-Edom for three months. During that time Obed-Edom and his family were greatly blessed, so David determined that it would now be safe to move the Ark again. This time David made sure that the proper rituals were being followed. He prepared a Tabernacle tent for it in Jerusalem. Then he assembled all of his people again, but told them that only the Levites could carry the Ark. The priests and the Levites sanctified themselves. The whole throng went as before, but the Levites assigned the proper musicians to sing and play the musical instruments. The Ark of the Covenant was retrieved from the house of Obed-Edom and carried on the shoulders of the Levites to the place that had been prepared for it in Jerusalem. David and thousands of others celebrated the movement of the Ark. David made burnt offerings to God and blessed his people. There was great rejoicing and dancing. David himself participated in praising God by dancing without restraint with his head and feet uncovered and wearing the priest's ephod. David returned to his household after the festivities, and was confronted by his wife Michal who had watched him dancing from her window and couldn't understand his complete elation. She castigated him for his undignified behavior. David responded by reminding her that God had chosen him, above her father Saul and all of her family, to be ruler over Israel.

David had intended that the Tabernacle tent would be a temporary place to hold the Ark of the Covenant, and he hoped to build a temple to be its more permanent home. He gathered materials and drew up plans for its construction. He told Nathan the prophet about his plans. Nathan told him that God had revealed that David's house and throne would be established forever, but that he would not be the one who would build the Temple. (2 Samuel 7:12-13)

Remembering his beloved friend Jonathan, David wondered whether there were any descendants of Saul to whom he could show kindness for Jonathan's sake. He asked Ziba, who had been one of Saul's servants. Ziba told him that Jonathan had a son Mephibosheth who was lame. Mephibosheth and his young son Micha were brought to the palace, and David restored to them the land that had been Saul's and instructed Ziba that he and his family should farm the land and be servants to Mephibosheth. Jonathan's son ate at the king's table from then on, with David's sons.

After coming to Jerusalem David had taken more concubines and had additional children. He also added another wife, Bathsheba, but the manner in which she became his wife is considered one of David's greatest sins. During one of Israel's conflicts David did not join his army in the battle, but remained in Jerusalem. One evening he was walking along the rooftop looking out over his city. From his vantage point he saw a beautiful woman bathing, and he inquired who she was.

He was told that she was Bathsheba, the wife of Uriah the Hittite. Uriah was away fighting in the war. David sent for Bathsheba. Some weeks later she told him that she was pregnant. Realizing that it would be obvious that he had committed adultery, he tried to hide his sin. He had Uriah called back from the battle. When Uriah arrived at the palace David inquired about how the fighting was progressing. Then he sent him to his own house to be with his wife, but Uriah did not go to his house. Instead, he slept by the door of the palace where David's servants slept because he did not think that it was proper for him to have the luxury and comfort of being with his wife while his officers and fellow warriors were enduring the hardships of war. When this scheme did not work, David sent Uriah back to the battlefront, but he also sent a letter to Joab directing him to place Uriah in the most dangerous part of the fighting so that he would be among those who would die. Uriah was killed in battle, and when Bathsheba learned that her husband was dead she mourned for him. When the period of mourning was past David sent for Bathsheba and she became his wife.

King David and Bathsheba were portrayed in this painting by Alexandr Andreevich Ivanov. (Wikimedia Commons)

After this, Nathan the prophet came to David and rebuked him and revealed God's displeasure with how David had broken His commandments. David sought forgiveness for his sin, and Nathan told him that God would forgive him but also punish him. He told him that the sword would never depart from his house and that rebellion within David's own family would occur as punishment. He also revealed that the baby that Bathsheba had conceived would not live. The baby died several days after its birth. (II Samuel 12:7-14)

It was Absalom, David's third son, who rebelled against his father, as was prophesied. Absalom's mother was Maachal, the daughter of the king of Geshur. Absalom was handsome, charming, and ambitious; and he undermined his father's power. David's love for his son made him oblivious to Absalom's covert plotting. After quietly building support throughout Israel, Absalom orchestrated a well-organized revolt from his headquarters in Hebron. David was taken by surprise and forced to flee from Jerusalem with a small following. He went into the wilderness to organize his defense. Absalom did take over Jerusalem temporarily, but was ultimately unable to prevail against his father's army. Despite Absalom's strong following, once David had gathered his supporters and loyal allies, his forces were able to completely rout Absalom's men in just one battle. David was advised not to accompany his army to the engagement in order to ensure his safety. He complied, but ordered them to spare Absalom. That was not to be. During the battle Absalom was caught by his hair in the branches of an oak tree, and killed by Joab and his armor bearers. When David was brought word of the successful defeat of the enemy, his first question was about the safety of Absalom. Hearing that his son had been killed he grieved greatly, and the day of victory was turned into a time of mourning.

As David grew older it was necessary for him to groom his successor. He had many sons who wanted to succeed him. Absalom had already unsuccessfully attempted to take over. Another son, Adonijah, was the son

This painting of King David in prayer was by Pieter de Grebber. (Wikimedia Commons)

of Haggith. He was David's fourth son, and being the oldest son still living he assumed that he should be the heir apparent. Joab supported him in this ambition, and when David was frail and seemed about to die Adonijah proclaimed himself king. Adonijah was not David's choice to be his successor.

Although David and his wife Bathsheba had a son that died soon after his birth, they also later had four more sons. The oldest of these sons was Solomon, and David had promised Bathsheba that Solomon would be king. Being aware of David's wishes, Bathsheba and Nathan the prophet visited David as he lay oblivious in his bed. They told him that Adonijah was claiming the kingship, and reminded him that he had selected Solomon to succeed him. David's consciousness was stirred, and he directed them to carry Solomon on the king's mule to Gihon, and for Zadok the priest and Nathan the prophet to anoint him king in front of the people. The instructions were followed and Solomon was proclaimed king in his father's stead, and the trumpets were blown and the people shouted, "God save the king." Adonijah heard the joyous commotion, and he and his followers accepted Solomon as king.

Before his death David instructed Solomon about the responsibilities he would have. He reminded him about keeping God's statutes, and he also directed him to seek vengeance against David's enemies and to treat kindly those who had been loyal to him. He also transferred to Solomon all of the plans he had made for the construction of the Temple for the Ark of the Covenant. David died soon after he proclaimed Solomon the new king. He was about seventy years old and had been king for forty years - seven years ruling over Judah in Hebron and thirty-three years ruling over the combined tribes of Israel in Jerusalem. He was buried in the City of David.

David had lived a long and momentous life. From a young shepherd boy he had been transformed into the most powerful ruler of his era and one of the most well-known figures of all time. The path he had to follow to get there was not an easy one. While just a young man he was identified as God's chosen one, and was anointed king by the prophet Samuel; but he had to wait many years and endure many hardships before he became king. He had to live as a fugitive for years as Saul pursued him relentlessly and tried to kill him. David was a skillful warrior, a talented musician, a loyal friend, and a gifted poet. Even when living in the wilderness as an outcast, his charisma and leadership qualities were evidenced by the large number of devoted followers who were attracted to his cause despite the dire circumstances. Once David became king he excelled as a ruler. He reunited the divided tribes of Israel and established Jerusalem as his capital. He developed Israel into the most powerful and highly-regarded nation of that time. He expanded the territorial boundaries of his kingdom and accumulated great wealth for his realm. Although his empire was continually involved in conflicts with neighboring nations, David's armies were victorious. David was a giant of history, but he also made serious mistakes and committed sins for which he sought God's forgiveness. He attributed all that he achieved to God's blessings, and always remembered that he prevailed because God was with him. His enduring faith in the grace of God is exemplified by one of his most famous poems:

> "The Lord is my shepherd; I shall not want. He maketh me to lie down in green pastures; he leadeth me beside the still waters. He restoreth my soul; he leadeth me in the paths of righteousness for his name's sake. Yea, though I walk through the valley of the shadow of death, I will fear no evil; for thou art with me; thy rod and thy staff they comfort me. Thou preparest a table before me in the presence of mine enemies; thou anointest my head with oil; my cup runneth over. Surely goodness and mercy shall follow me all the days of my life; and I will dwell in the house of the Lord for ever." (Psalms: 23)

King David of Israel was promised by God that "thine house and thine kingdom shall be established for ever before thee: thy throne shall be established for ever." (2 Samuel 7:16) The promise has been kept. For over four hundred years there was a king of Judah upon the Throne of David, ending in 586 B.C. when Zedekiah and all of his sons were captured and removed by Nebuchadnezzar. Since that time there has not been a king of

Judah. However, the Throne of David, as prophesied, is ongoing and will last forever.

After the death of David, his son Solomon became king of Judah and Israel. Solomon reigned for forty years, and during that period of time his kingdom prospered, both materially and culturally. He built the Temple to house the Ark of the Covenant. Numerous other enormous construction projects were completed, resulting in examples of architectural splendor, improved military fortifications, and enhanced infrastructure. Commerce flourished. Solomon's fame spread, and he was renowned for his wisdom. He wrote proverbs which are recorded in the Old Testament. His vast realm exuded wealth and grandeur. His personal court included hundreds of wives and concubines, many of whom worshiped idols and did not follow God's laws. Solomon himself strayed from God's laws. During Solomon's rule Israel reached great heights, but in achieving those successes he produced discontent among those who were heavily taxed and those who resented the preferential treatment given to the House of Judah. By the end of his reign the kingdom had started to collapse.

When Solomon died his son Rehoboam became king, but he did not remain king of the entire Twelve Tribes of Israel. The ten northern tribes withdrew from the original kingdom that had been joined together under King David. They formed their own Kingdom of Israel with a capital in Samaria. This northern kingdom was eventually conquered by the Assyrians, and the descendants of those ten northern tribes became spread out and scattered, becoming the Ten Lost Tribes of Israel. Only the tribes of Judah and Benjamin continued to be loyal to Solomon's successor. They inhabited the southern part of the former kingdom and had their capital in Jerusalem. The Kingdom of Judah was further weakened when parts of it were conquered by invaders.

Members of the royal line of David continued to rule through fifteen more monarchies, though they did not preside over kingdoms as large and prosperous as David and Solomon had led. During those years the Kingdom

This is a map of the Holy Land by Jacobus Tirinus. (Wikimedia Commons)

of Judah was often in a very unstable condition and at different periods was a vassal state to Assyria, Egypt, or Babylon. In 597 B.C. Zedekiah, a direct descendent of David, was installed as king by Nebuchadnezzar II of Babylon. He would prove to be the last king of Judah.

During this era the prophet Jeremiah continually warned the inhabitants of the Kingdom of Judah that they must return to obeying the Covenant that had been made with God in order to avoid destruction. Jeremiah began his prophecies during the reign of King Josiah, around 625 B.C. Josiah was a pious king who enacted religious reforms to return his people to strict obedience to God's laws. He also ruled over the Kingdom of Judah during a period in which his country could govern itself without foreign interference. After Josiah's death in battle it was not long before his kingdom was no longer independent. During his sons' reigns the Egyptians and then the Babylonians took control, although the sons were still officially the rulers. The Kingdom of Judah reverted once again to idolatry and immorality. Jeremiah spoke courageously and repeatedly to the people of Jerusalem, warning them of the dangers that were imminent if they did not repent.

When Zedekiah, the last son of Josiah to become king, failed to heed his warnings and rebelled against Babylon, Jeremiah admonished him that God was sending Nebuchadnezzar to punish the Kingdom of Judah and that the

Baruch recorded Jeremiah's prophecies, as in Jeremiah 36:4. (Wikimedia Commons)

only chance for survival was to submit to the Babylonians. Zedekiah still did not follow Jeremiah's advice, and imprisoned him instead. Then Zedekiah tried unsuccessfully to enlist the help of the Egyptians, and when that failed Nebuchadnezzar's army was able to besiege Jerusalem. The siege lasted about a year and a half. By then Jerusalem and its inhabitants were so weakened that the Babylonians were able to break through the walls of the city. Zedekiah tried to escape with his sons, but was captured. His sons were killed in front of him, and then he was blinded and imprisoned for the rest of his life. There would be no more kings of Judah. (Jeremiah 39:6-7, 52:10-11)

The city of Jerusalem, including the magnificent Temple that Solomon had built, was destroyed in 586 B.C. Many of the people of Jerusalem who were not killed were taken captive, but some of the poor people were allowed to remain and tend to the vineyards and fields. Nebuchadnezzar ordered his captain of the guard to free Jeremiah so that he could be among his people.

Jeremiah's prophecies had come to pass, but his work was not done. He had been enabled to speak God's words, but he was also commissioned to be an agent to bring about God's plan. Jeremiah reports in the Bible that "the Lord put forth his hand, and touched my mouth. And the Lord said unto me, Behold, I have put my words in thy mouth. See, I have this day set thee over the nations and over the kingdoms, to root out, and to pull down, and to destroy, and to throw down, to build, and to plant." (Jeremiah 1:9-10) Jeremiah prophesied about and witnessed the destruction of his nation, but his role in building and planting was yet to reveal itself.

During the capture of Jerusalem Jeremiah had protected the daughters of Zedekiah, and also some precious historical relics from the Temple. After the invaders had left he remained near Jerusalem for a while consoling and encouraging the limited number of people who had survived. Nebuchadnezzar had installed Gedaliah as governor and placed him in charge of those who remained after the destruction of Jerusalem. Gedaliah resided in Mizpah, and it was there that Jeremiah and his people lived. Their numbers grew as others, realizing that a remnant of Judah remained in the care of the governor, returned to join them. However, the security that Gedaliah provided did not last for long. He and many of the people with him were killed by Ishmael and his forces. Others were carried away as captives. They were apprehended by Johanan and his men, and the captives were released. Johanan urged all of the people to go to Egypt for safety. Jeremiah prophesied against going into Egypt, but his warnings were ignored and he, the king's daughters, and Baruch, his scribe, were taken forcibly into Egypt. (Jeremiah 43:6-7) They remained there in Tahpanphes for a while, but then Jeremiah was warned by God that Nebuchadnezzar was about to invade Egypt. Realizing that it would no longer be safe there, he and a small group (including Baruch and one of Zedekiah's daughters, Princess Tephi) fled aboard a Phoenician ship. As it had been prophesied: "And the remnant that is escaped of the house of Judah shall again take root downward, and bear fruit upward: For out of Jerusalem shall go forth a remnant..." (Isaiah 37:31-32) They took with them the relics that Jeremiah had saved from the destruction of the Temple, including the harp of David, and the Stone of Destiny which was the stone pillow that Jacob had slept on as he dreamed of Jacob's ladder. (Genesis 28:10-22)

Some scholars believe that the Ark of the Covenant was one of the relics that Jeremiah carried with him when he fled Egypt, but Jeremiah indicated that God did not think it was still important and it appears that Jeremiah did not feel any need to save it. (Jeremiah 3:16)

There are many theories that have been espoused over the centuries concerning the whereabouts of the Ark of the Covenant. One theory is that it is located in a desert site in Yemen known as Marib. Another idea is that it is hidden in the Temple Mount in Jerusalem. Some feel that it is in Egypt in the Great Pyramid of Giza. Another theory is that it is in the Church of Our Lady Mary of Zion in Axum, Ethiopia. Still another belief is that the Ark of the Covenant was brought back by Knights Templar during one of the crusades and then hidden in central England or in Lanquedoc, France. Another theory is that it was taken by Jeremiah to Tara in County Meath in Ireland. However, Jeremiah prophesied: "And it shall come to pass, when ye be multiplied and increased in the land, in those days, saith the Lord, they shall say no more, The ark of the covenant of the Lord: neither shall it come to mind: neither shall they remember it..." (Jeremiah 3:16)

Jeremiah and his companions traveled across the Mediterranean Sea, stopping in Gibraltar and Spain, and eventually arrived in a bay off Cornwall at the southwest tip of what is now England. Then they sailed to their intended destination on the eastern side of what is now Ireland. They were met there by Oilioll who would become the husband of Princess Tephi.

This map has been modified to show the route of Princess Tephi and Jeremiah from Jerusalem to Tara and Teltown in Hibernia, with stops in Egypt, Gibraltar, Spain, and Britain. (Wikimedia Commons)

Oilioll (also known as Eochaidh [knight] and Heremon [high king]) was a descendant of Judah, through Judah's son Zerah. Judah was the fourth son of Jacob and the founder of one of the Twelve Tribes of Israel. Jacob had blessed each of his sons, as he was about to die. His words to Judah were: "Judah, thou art he whom thy brethren shall praise....Judah is a lion's whelp....The scepter shall not depart from Judah, nor a lawgiver from between his feet, until Shiloh (generally thought to be either peace or The Messiah who would rule the united tribes of Israel as king) come...." (Genesis 49:8 -10) Judah had twin sons, Pharez and Zerah. At the time of their birth the midwife tied a red string around the wrist of the first hand that appeared during their births, in order to mark the firstborn. As soon as she had done that, though, the hand was withdrawn, and the other baby actually was born first. The baby with the red string was named Zerah, and his brother was named Pharez. Pharez received the rights inherent to the firstborn. It was from Pharez's line that David and Solomon and the successive kings of Judah emerged. Zerah eventually traveled away to establish his own line in exile. The line of Zerah continued on through the generations, but not in the land of Judah. His descendants continued to move on and many ultimately settled in Hibernia, which is now called Ireland. It was there that Oilioll lived.

Not long after Princess Tephi arrived in 583 B.C., her marriage to Oilioll was arranged. Princess Tephi, being the daughter of Zedekiah, was in the royal line of David descending from Judah's son Pharez. Oilioll was a descendant of Gallam, a Milesian prince, whose direct line went back to Calcol, who was one of the sons of Judah's son Zerah. Their marriage would accomplish miraculous things. It would heal the breach between the two lines of Judah and ensure that the scepter would not depart from Judah. The future monarchs descended from Oilioll and Princess Tephi would carry on the Davidic Bloodline (Numbers 36:6-9) and the Throne of David forever. (2 Samuel 7:16) The transfer of power from the Pharez line of Judah to the Zerah line of Judah which resulted from their marriage would fulfill Ezekiel's prophecy (Ezekiel 17). In addition, Jeremiah's commission "to build, and to plant" would be achieved by his having brought Zedekiah's daughter, Princess Tephi, safely to Hibernia and having overseen her marriage to Oilioll the Zerahite upon the sacred Stone of Destiny in 583 B.C.

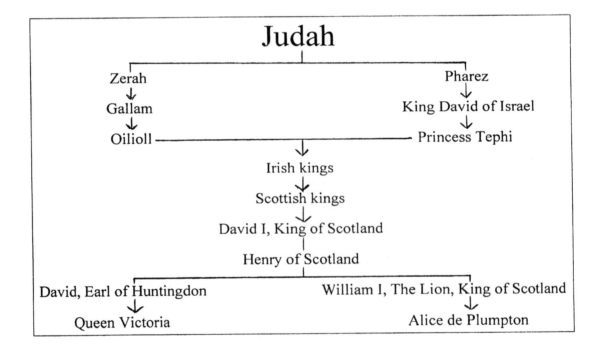

This chart, by Robert H. Nelson, shows the lines coming down from Zerah and Pharez.

The descendants of Oilioll and Princess Tephi, carrying both the royal line of Judah and the Davidic Bloodline, continued through the Irish kings, then the Scottish kings, and later to the monarchs of England. Alice de Plumpton had direct ancestors who carried the Davidic Bloodline down to her and after her to all of her descendants, and those ancestors shared the royal line of Judah for over 2,100 years until her ancestral line reached Henry of Scotland, the son of David I, King of Scotland.

The line of Queen Victoria and ultimately Queen Elizabeth II continued down to them through Henry's son, David, Earl of Huntingdon. The line of Alice de Plumpton continued down to her through Henry's son, William I, The Lion, King of Scotland.

King David of Israel

Solomon

Rehoboam

Abijam

Asa

Jehoshaphat

Jehoram

Ahaziah

Joash

Amaziah

Uzziah

Jotham

Ahaz

Hezekiah

Manasseh

Amon

Josiah

Zedekiah

Princess Tephi

Giallchadh

Nuahas Fionn Fail

Aodhain Glas

Simeon Breac

Muireadach Bolgrach

Fiachadh Tolgrach

Duach Laidrach

Eochaidh Buaigllorg

Ugaine Mor

Cobhthach Coalbreag

Meilage

Jaran Fathach

Conla Caomb

Olioll Caisfhiachach

Eochaidh Alethair

Aengus Tuirmheach Teamharch

Eana Aighneach

Labhra

Blathachtach

Eassmain Eamhna

Roighnein Ruadh

Fionnlogh

Fionn

Eochaidh Feidhlioch

Fineamhuas

Lughaidh

Criomthan Niadhnar

Fearaidhach Fion-Feachtnuigh

Fiachadh Fionoluidh

Tuathal Teachtmar

Fedlimid Rachtmar

Coun Ceadchathach

Airt Aonthir

Cormac Ulfhota

Caibre Liffeachair

Fiachadh Sreabthuine

Muireadhach Tireach

Eochaid Moigmeodhin

Niall

Eogan

Muireadhach

Fergus Mor

Domangart

Gabran

Aidan

Eochaid

Domnall

Domangart

Eochaid

Eochaid

Aedh

Eochaid

Alpin

Kenneth I

Constantin I

Donald II

Malcolm I

Kenneth II

Malcolm II

Bethoc

Duncan I

Malcolm III

David I, King of Scotland

Henry of Scotland

William I, The Lion, King of Scotland

Isabella of Scotland

William de Ros

William de Ros

Lucy de Ros

William de Plumpton

Alice de Plumpton

Abbot, Jacob. *William the Conqueror*. New York: Harper & Brothers Publishers, 1901.

Addison, C. E. *The Temple Church*. London: Longman, Brown, Green and Longmans, 1843.

Allen, J. H. *Judah's Scepter and Joseph's Birthright*. Boston: A. A. Beauchamp, 1917.

Baronii, Caesaris S.R.E. Card. *Annales Ecclesiastici*. Parisiis: Barri-Ducis, MDCCCLXIV.

Bury, J.B. *The Cambridge Medieval History*. New York: The MacMillan Company, 1913.

Carpenter, William. *The Israelites Found in the Anglo-Saxons*. London: George Kenning, 1872.

Cox, George William. *The Crusades*. London: Longmans, Green, and Co, 1875.

Cutts, Edward L. *Charlemagne*. London: Society for Promoting Christian Knowledge, 1882.

Eginhard. *Life of Charlemagne* (translated from the text of the *Monumenta Germaniae* by S. E. Turner). New York: American Book Company, 1880.

Elliott, Charles. *Old Testament Prophecy*. New York: A. C. Armstrong and Son, 1889.

Encyclopaedia Britannica (Eleventh Edition). New York: The Encyclopaedia Britannica Company, 1910.

The Encyclopedia Americana. New York: The Encyclopedia Americana Corporation, 1919.

French, George Russell. *The Ancestry of Her Majesty Queen Victoria, and of His Royal Highness Prince Albert*. London: William Pickering, 1841.

Fuller, Thomas. *The Church History of Britain*. London: Thomas Tegg and Son, 1837.

Garretson, Arthur Samuel. *Primitive Christianity and Early Criticisms*. Boston: Sherman, French & Company, 1912.

Gibbon, Edward. *The History of the Decline and Fall of the Roman Empire*. London: Methuen & Co., 1900.

Gray, Andrew. *The Origin and Early History of Christianity in Britain.* London: Skeffington & Son, 1897.

Haaren, John H., and Poland, A. B. *Famous Men of the Middle Ages*. New York: American Book Company, 1904.

The Holy Bible Containing the Old and New Testaments (King James Version). Glasgow: Printers for the Queen in Scotland, 1839.

Lang, Andrew. *A Short History of Scotland.* New York: Dodd, Mead and Company, 1912.

Lansing, Marion Florence. *Barbarian and Noble*. Boston: Ginn and Company, 1911.

Lees, Beatrice Adelaide. *Alfred the Great, The Truth Teller*, *Maker of England*, *848-899*. New York: G. P. Putnam's Sons, 1915.

Lewis, Abram Herbert. *Paganism Surviving in Christianity*. New York: G. P. Putnam's Sons, 1892.

Lewis, Lionel Smithett. *St. Joseph of Arimathea at Glastonbury*. London: A.R. Mowbray, 1922.

Marti, Karl. *The Religion of the Old Testament*. London: Williams & Norgate, 1907.

Mawer, Allen. *The Vikings*. Cambridge: The Cambridge University Press, 1913.

McKechnie, William Sharp. *Magna Charta: A Commentary on the Great Charter of King John.* Glasgow: James MacLehose and Sons, 1905.

Meyer, Paul. *L'Histoire de Guillaume le Marechal*. Nogent-Le-Rotrou: Imprimerie Daupeley-Gouverneur, 1882.

Morgan, R.W. *St. Paul in Britain; or, The Origin of British as Opposed to Papal Christianity*. London: J.H. and Jas. Parker, 1900.

Newton, Benjamin Wills. *David The King of Israel*. London: Houlston and Sons, 1874.

Norgate, Kate. *The Minority of Henry the Third*. London: MacMillan and Co., 1912.

Orr, James. *The International Standard Bible Encyclopaedia*. Chicago: The Howard-Severance Company, 1915.

Rogers, Ellen M. The *Coronation Stone and England's Interest In It*. London: James Nisbet & Co., 1881.

Sanders, Frank Knight. *History of the Hebrews*. New York: Charles Scribner's Sons, 1914.

Stevenson, William Henry, ed. *Asser's Life of King Alfred* (originally written in Latin in 893). Oxford: The Clarendon Press, 1904.

Tappan, Eva March. *European Hero Stories*. Boston: Houghton Mifflin Company, 1909.

Taylor, John William. *The Coming of the Saints*. London: Methuen & Company, 1906.

Taylor, Robert. *The Diegesis; Being a Discovery of the Origin, Evidences, and Early History of Christianity*. London: Richard Carlile, 1829.

Totten, Charles Adiel Lewis. *The Early Story of Ireland*. New Haven: Our Race Publishing Company, 1905.

Turner, Sharon. *The History of England During the Middle Ages*. London: Longman, Brown, Green, and Longmans, 1853.

Wikimedia Commons, an online repository of free-use images. (commons.wikimedia.org)

Wild, Joseph. *The Lost Ten Tribes*. Boston: A. A. Beauchamp, 1919.

The Authors

Robert H. Nelson and Emma L. Nelson

FromGreatMen@gmail.com

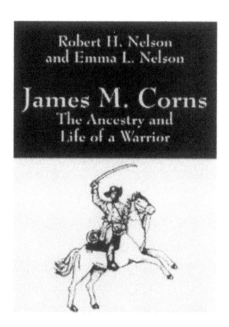

James M. Corns, born in 1830, was descended from prominent families in Staffordshire and Gloucestershire, England. While living as a child in Monmouthshire, his father died and then his mother abandoned him when she remarried. From those sad and unpromising circumstances he rose to become the commander of the 8th Virginia Cavalry Regiment of the Confederate States of America. He was called everything from "a gallant officer, a very intelligent gentleman" to "a drinking blackguard." After the war his wife deserted him and took their seven children into Pennsylvania and out of his reach. He then headed into the "wild West" building the railroads, and later was an architect and builder with a thriving business in East Texas. He found a new wife and had a bigamous marriage in Texas and Louisiana. The remarkable story of the life of James M. Corns, the defeats he suffered and his ability to keep up the fight even when faced with overwhelming losses, is a story of resilience, perseverance, courage, and talent. The life of James M. Corns was truly the life of a warrior.

Read in this factual, carefully sourced book about the family lines that created him and his amazing life in and out of the military.

The authors, Robert H. Nelson (a great-great-grandson of James M. Corns) and his wife Emma L. Nelson, have researched the ancestry and life of James M. Corns for over 40 years and have traveled widely to put his story together. They have utilized writings from his time, extensive National Archives records, and family letters and documents; and they have depicted his ancestry and life in this definitive biography. Bob and Emmy Lou "wrote the book" on James M. Corns.

> "The authors of the book 'James M. Corns: The Ancestry and Life of a Warrior,' did a superior job of describing the fascinating life of one of their forefathers. James M. Corns led a heroic and, at times, tragic life that was beautifully depicted in historical dialogue and documentation, including family letters, maps, photographs, and records from the National Archives. Anyone who enjoys reading a factual account about Civil War (a.k.a. The War in Defense of Virginia) history will cherish the depth and texture of this amazing book."

> "Robert and Emma have done a great job in pulling this book together on the family history, life and times of James M. Corns. I too am a family history researcher and a member of the Corns family through marriage. Every researcher always ends up having favorite ancestors and you are always hoping one will be interesting and colorful. Col. James M. Corns' life was that and so much more to all his descendants. Robert and Emma Nelson have done their "homework" in their research. It's obvious to the reader it was a true labor of love for both of them. I think the Colonel would be pleased with this book."

Lightning Source UK Ltd.
Milton Keynes UK
UKHW051854110219
337105UK00001B/7/P

9 781432 779139